Pregnancy

The Best Time to Submerge Your Baby in Prayer

ISBN: Softcover   978-1-951313-02-9
         Hardcover   978-1-951313-03-6
         eBook   978-1-951313-04-3

Published in the United States of America.

Black Lacquer Press & Marketing Inc.
3225 McLeod Drive
Suite 100
Las Vegas, Nevada 89121
USA
www.blacklacquerpress.net

Quantity sales. Special discounts are available on quantity purchases by corporations, associations, and others. For details, contact the publisher at the address above.

To:

_____

From:

_____

Date:

_____

in honor of your conception.

Contents

Acknowledgements

There are so many special people who believed in this project and accompanied me throughout the journey that culminated in the production and translation of this book.

My sincere thanks to:

Lillian López, my sister in Christ, for being my prayer partner, for believing in this project when it was just a dream, for accompanying and encouraging me from the beginning to the end.

Nyrma Feliciano, my covenant sister, for covering me in prayer, for contributing her knowledge of medicine, for reading the draft and for the valuable recommendations made in the process.

Carmen Marchany, my spiritual daughter, who assumed various roles in the process. She held me up with her prayers, contributed ideas and assumed the arduous task of editing the Spanish manuscript.

María S Pedraza, my sister in Christ, who by her own initiative said, "Here I am" and assumed full responsibility for organizing the format of the Spanish manuscript.

Sara Arroyo, my sister in Christ, for the hours invested in the first edition of the Spanish manuscript.

The Squadron of forty prayer warriors from my church, for adopting one of the forty weeks of pregnancy and covering it with prayer.

Pastor Oscar Rivera, physician, who provided information on the function of the organs of the baby and also a member of the prayer squadron.

Ruth Sanjurjo, for the many tasks she assumed, contributing her artistic ideas, advice and help in formatting the final Spanish manuscript.

Wanda Soler, my spiritual daughter, for sharing her valuable writer's advice and her emotional support.

Edwin Correa, for designing the book cover.

Judy Cox, my sister, for reviewing the initial translation from Spanish to English.

Tony Oliveras, for the full translation of the book from Spanish to English.

Rafael Flores, for his assistance in the initial editing of the translation from Spanish to English.

Angélica Cid, my sister, who took upon herself the responsibility of typing all of the English manuscript, and for the hundreds of hours she invested in editing the final version of the English translation.

Luis Cid, my brother in-law, for supporting his wife, Angelica Cid, during the long hours of the editing process and for also proofreading the final manuscript.

Loida Levy, my sister, for proofreading the final manuscript of the English translation.

Dedication

I dedicate this book, first and foremost, to the Holy Spirit, the true author. The one, who inspired me, pushed and sustained me through the long process of completing it.

Secondly, to Andrés Rivera Chico, the child with whom some of the principles in this book were first used when his mother was pregnant. Today Andrés is a young teen who, from his childhood, knows the scriptures and enjoys an intimate relationship with God. Andrés knows his destiny in God! He speaks passionately about his need to prepare himself to take the Word of God to the nations.

"These commandments that I give you today are to be upon your hearts. Impress them on your children. Talk about them when you sit at home and when you walk along the road, when you lie down and when you get up."

Deuteronomy 6:6–7(NIV)

Prologue

"From birth I was cast on you; from my mother's womb you have been my God."

Psalm 22:10 (NIV)

The exclamation in Psalm 22:10 perfectly portrays the purpose of this book: To help parents use the 40 weeks of gestation to submerge their unborn child in the Word of God. Just as the baby's umbilical cord nourishes his physical body, the Word of God becomes his lifeline to his Creator; saturating his spiritual senses, so he may come to long for the pure milk of the Word of God, and by it he may grow in respect to salvation (1 Peter 2:2). Science is just beginning to explain how it is possible for there to be multiple cases of persons who have memories of experiences that took place while they were still in their mother's womb. The prominent Dr. Thomas Verny in his book: *The Secret Life of the Unborn Child*, (1988) presents numerous examples of these cases from different parts of the world. Interestingly, Dr. Verny also presents evidence of how a baby from its mother's womb knows if he is a wanted baby or not, and the effect that this has on him in his adult life.

In line with these investigations the fields of prenatal and perinatal psychology have emerged. These are interdisciplinary studies of the foundations of health in body, mind, emotions and in enduring response patterns to life. They are the study of the psychological and psychophysiological effects and implications of the earliest experiences of the individual before birth (prenatal), as well as during and immediately after childbirth (perinatal), on the health and learning ability of the individual and on their social relationships.

Research has confirmed some of the experiences the baby has in the womb are being imprinted in his inner being. It has also confirmed, beyond a doubt, that during the process of gestation, the baby can hear, see, feel and react to stimuli from the outside world as John the Baptist did while he was still inside his mother's womb.

Based on these scientific findings, I ask myself if in 2nd Tim 3:15 the Bible is referring to Timothy's prenatal memory in the same way Isaiah 40:22 makes reference to the world being round, long before Christopher Columbus made this discovery. In 2nd Timothy 3:15, it says that from his childhood Timothy knew the scriptures. What's interesting in this Bible verse is that when you study it in its original language, the word childhood can also mean: "*typically an infant that has not been born.*" With this in mind, 2nd Timothy 3:15 can be paraphrased to read: *and while you were in your mother's womb, you have known the Holy Scriptures (Author emphasis).* Could it be that his grandmother Lois, and Eunice, his mother, took a proactive approach and used the time of gestation to begin to teach Timothy the scriptures, as they also developed a bonding relationship with him from the very womb?

The time has come for the people of God to apply the knowledge in the field of prenatal memory in conjunction with the Word of God to instruct their unborn child on its identity in Jesus Christ during the pregnancy period. This book does precisely that; it combines the Word of God and the findings of science concerning prenatal memory. The intent is for parents to have a tool that will not limit them to only praying for the physical development of the baby in gestation, but also have a tool to help them pray for the unborn child's soul and spirit. As a result of the Word of God being imprinted in the baby's inner being, his spiritual senses will begin to develop, sharpen and lead him, at a very early age, to an intimate relationship with his Creator and a victorious life in Christ Jesus.

I firmly believe this book reflects God's heart for a time such as this. The Bible is definitely the greatest teaching manual in existence and science continues to confirm the veracity of what has been written in its pages. Pregnancy is a vital time in the life of the parents and the unborn child. Don't miss the opportunity and privilege you have as parents to enter into an alliance with God to declare life upon the spirit, soul and body of your unborn child.

Introduction

*"So is my word that goes out from my mouth: It will not return
to me empty, but will accomplish what I desire and achieve the
purpose for which I sent it."*

Isaiah 55:11

The purpose of this book is to connect your baby to the powerful
Word of God during the entire gestation period. It links the principles
of the Bible with scientific findings on prenatal memory. The goal
is that as you submerge your baby in prayers, based on the Bible,
the Word will imprint itself in his inner being, sharpen his spiritual
senses, and pave the way for him to enjoy an intimate relationship
with God at an early age and live a victorious life in Christ Jesus.

It is a tool to help you take advantage of the nine months of pregnancy
to develop a bonding relationship with your baby as you wrap him
in God's love. The Bible teaches us in 1ˢᵗ Thessalonians 5:23 that we
are spirit, soul and body and the three should be sanctified. For this
reason, prayers have been included so you can sanctify and nourish
these three essential aspects of your baby's development.

Pregnancy is definitely the best time to begin praying for your baby.
The baby is captive inside its mother's womb for nine months. In a
mysterious way, for good or for evil, the experiences around him are
being imprinted in his inner being. This book will help you imprint
experiences of life, which will prepare him for his life in the world.
It is not about making positive statements, rather prayers based on
Biblical principles. It is about blessing your baby with the power of

the Word which is living and active and sharper than a two-edged sword, piercing as far as the division of soul and spirit, of both joints and marrow, and able to judge the thoughts and intentions of the heart. *(Hebrews 4:12)*

The first page provides a place for you to dedicate this book to the baby you will be praying for. You can choose to give it to the baby once he is born or wait until he is old enough to value it. A gift like this is a treasure that conveys the message that someone loved him so much that, week after week, they took the time to pray for his physical development and to nourish his soul and spirit with the Word of God. Can you imagine the effect an act like this, combined with your prayers, will have on the emotional development of the child in the coming years?

Beginning with the period *before* pregnancy, prayers are provided for the couple to consecrate the ovum and the sperm that will unite to conceive their baby. It also includes a prayer to sustain the couple if the period of conception is prolonged.

A very special section has been included which compiles the findings of the Messianic Jew, Zola Levitt. Mr. Levitt unveils, in an impressive way, how our God has interwoven the pregnancy process with the Feasts of Israel described in the book of Leviticus. This information has been summarized in tables and is located in the corresponding month of pregnancy. If you wish to read more on this matter, visit the webpage: *www.levitte.com* and request the video: *A Child is Born* or the pamphlet: *The Seven Feasts of Israel.*

For ease of use, the contents have been organized around the nine months of pregnancy and the weeks that make up the month. In each table you will discover the prayer focus for each month, the name of God used, and the relation between the week of pregnancy and the Feasts of Israel.

In the section, *I Am Alive and I Describe My Physical Development*, the baby describes himself in a joyful and sometimes amusing way. He speaks to his parents about his physical development during that week and glorifies God for the care he has received from him. This book does not pretend to be a medical manual, but rather an avenue for a pleasant dialogue between the parents and their unborn child.

The section, *Prayer Guide for the Physical Development of Our Baby*, begins before the pregnancy has occurred. It starts with prayer to sanctify the ovum and the sperm that will unite at the moment of conception. If the pregnancy is delayed, you will find a prayer to sustain both the husband and the wife during the waiting period of the conception of their baby. Once the baby is conceived, there is a prayer for each week of pregnancy. The prayers in this section present to the Lord each organ in development that week and its function.

The section, *Prayer Guide for the Soul of Our Baby (emotions – mind – will)*, provides the parents with the opportunity for planting the powerful Word of God in the baby's soul, as it grows in the mother's womb. Given that the Word teaches us in Psalm 8:2 that from the mouth of infants and nursing babies, God established strength. This, without a doubt, is the best time to begin to pray for the soul of your baby. The nine manifestations of the fruit of the Holy Spirit have been integrated into the prayers for the soul. Furthermore, each week a Bible character has been identified who exhibited this fruit. You are invited to pray with the conviction that you will have guaranteed results; for the Word of God never comes back empty, but it accomplishes that for which it was sent (*Isaiah 55:11*). In these prayers, you will be asking God to give the baby a heart conformed to his, to make him wise and to fill him with his intelligence.

The section, **Prayer Guide for the Spirit of Our Baby,** follows the same pattern, based on the Word of God, prophesying and blessing the spirit of the baby, but with a slightly different approach. With these prayers you will speak directly to the baby's spirit and begin to instruct him on how much God loves him, his identity in God, his unique ability to discern the things of God, and to be able to communicate directly with God. The ultimate goal of the prayers for the spirit is to begin to fine tune your baby's spiritual senses as you feed him with the beautiful and powerful Word of God. As you speak to your baby's spirit, while he is still in the womb, you will be instructing him on his inheritance in God, the need for him to surrender his heart to Jesus, his spiritual senses, each piece of the armor of God and the gifts of the spirit that are available to him.

The appendix includes several important resources, such as a quick reference that allows you to know at a glance, the name of God that is used, the prayer focus and the Bible character chosen for that week. It also includes a guide and prayer to be used when, for some reason, *the baby was not initially wanted.* You will find a prayer guide for *those who have lived the experience of an abortion* and a prayer guide in case that during the pregnancy you suffer *the loss of your baby.* These prayers should not be turned into a tedious ritual. Rather, it should be a delightful experience where parents can enjoy some beautiful moments of intimacy with their baby. Do not think that in one day you have to read all the prayers assigned to a week. The prayers can be divided as follows:

Day 1: Read the section where the baby describes his development. Afterwards, talk with your baby about what has been read and the joy of having him.

Day 2: Read the section on the prayer for the physical development of the baby.

Day 3: Read the section on the prayer for the baby's soul.

Day 4: Read the section on the prayer for the baby's spirit.

Day 5: You can re-read the section of the prayers for the physical development of the baby and add other blessings.

Day 6: You can re-read the section of the prayers for the soul and add other blessings.

Day 7: You can re-read the section of the prayers for the baby's spirit and add other blessings.

What's important is for both parents to enjoy these lovely moments together with their baby and simultaneously begin to bond with their child. This does not imply that if the parents are separated during the period of gestation, they cannot use this book. On the contrary, it provides an opportunity for the father or the mother, on their own, to learn about their baby's development and to begin establishing a deep bonding relationship with their unborn child as they pray for him each week. Likewise, these prayers can be said by grandparents, uncles, aunts, or anyone else willing to take the responsibility of submerging a child in prayer and become part of the formation of the identity of Christ in the child.

Although this book starts with the period before pregnancy, you can begin to use it during any of the forty weeks of the baby's gestation. As a matter of fact, the prayers for the soul and spirit have the peculiarity that they can be used to pray for your grandchildren, nieces, nephews, brothers, sisters or any other loved one, regardless of their age.

Since this book will be used to pray for male and female babies and because, initially, the gender of the baby is unknown, I have used the neutral term, your baby instead of him or her. However, this was not always possible, in which case I used the term he or it. My recommendation is that once you know your baby's gender, you personalize your prayers. When you know the name the baby will receive, use the baby's name.

First Month

Weeks 1-4

Summary of the Pregnancy Process

Weeks 1-2: Preconception: To create a certain consistency, doctors calculate pregnancy from the first day of the last menstrual cycle. The ovum is released fourteen days after the start of the menstrual cycle.

Week 3: The ovum is fertilized and conception takes place.

Week 4: The fertilized ovum travels to the uterus where it will be implanted.

The Prayer Focus Will Be:

Week	Name of God	Bible Character	Prayer Focus The Soul	Prayer Focus The Spirit
1. **Preconception** Time of joy and expectation of conception.	Creator	Jesus, the Messiah	N/A	N/A
2. **Preconception** Time of joy and waiting to conceive.	The Highest	Isaac	N/A	N/A
3.	The Potter	Elizabeth	The Fruit of Love	Identity in God
4.	The Good Shepherd	Jonathan	The Fruit of Love	Identity in God

The Festivals of Israel and Pregnancy

The Festivals of Israel	Pregnancy
The Jewish calendar has approximately 280 days.	The term of the pregnancy is approximately 280 days.
The Passover Feast – Selection of the Lamb Lev 23:5: "In the first month, on the fourteenth day of the month, at twilight, is the LORD's Passover."	**Preconception – Ovulation** Fourteen days after the start of the menstrual cycle, the ovary releases an ovum.
The Feast of Unleavened Bread Lev 23:6: "Then on the fifteenth day of the same month is the Feast of Unleavened Bread to the LORD; for seven days you shall eat unleavened bread."	**Fertilization – Conception** Fertilization of the ovum must occur within 24 hours of its release from the ovary, on the 15th day of the same month.
The Feast of First Fruits (Lev 23:10-14) It is celebrated on first Sunday of the week of the Feast of Unleavened Bread. It could be from 2 to 6 days.	**Implant of Fertilized Ovum** The fertilized ovum travels down at its own pace. It doesn't have a specific time cycle. It can take from 2 to 6 days for the implant to occur.

Week 1: Preconception: The baby rejoices upon the expectation of being conceived.

Hi, it's me, your baby! The baby you have been thinking about. I feel so special. Why shouldn't I feel special? I'm not an accident. My God, the Creator of the universe chose me before the creation of the world. I am the Creator's beautiful design and poem. I will come into the world to do good deeds in Jesus Christ, which he prepared for me to walk in. Hallelujah! I come with a destiny and fully equipped to fulfill it.

I'm very smart; so let me tell you how things are from my point of view. Doctors, as well as my Creator, call things that don't exist as if they already existed. They calculate the 40 weeks of pregnancy based on the first day of Mommy's last menstrual cycle. So, Mommy and Daddy listen carefully; I'm going to give you a short lesson on biology. The average woman menstruates every 28 days. The first day of her cycle begins when she observes her menstrual flow. The period lasts a few days. Something wonderful, called ovulation, occurs on the 14th day after the start of the menstruation period. The highest probability of my being conceived is during ovulation, when Mommy's ovary releases an ovum. Here comes the interesting part. If only one of Daddy's 500 million spermatozoids succeeds in penetrating Mommy's ovum, they will embrace each other and I will have been conceived.

You will agree with me that my Creator is brilliant! With great love and care he created man and woman with the ability to unite and procreate. He deposited sperm in the man, the smallest cell in the body, which has half of everything necessary to give me life. In the woman he deposited ovum, the largest cell in the body, which possesses the other half of what is needed to conceive life. All this so conception would occur as the product of the union of a man and a woman.

My Creator knows it all! Listen to what he says about me: "Before I formed you in the womb, I knew you, and before you were born,

I consecrated you; my substance was not hidden from you when I was secretly wrought and made in the lowest parts of the earth!" Hallelujah! The Creator of the universe knows who I am and with great attention fixed his eyes on me. I will come to this world with a well-defined destiny and purpose. My Creator will carefully choose the 23 pairs of chromosomes and over 10,000 genes which will form my physical body. Each part of my inheritance will be majestically interwoven. He will make sure I have everything necessary to be a conqueror and fulfill the purpose for which I am being created.

The Couple Pray Using The Scriptures To Procreate A Baby

Beloved Creator, we thank you because being you, the giver of life, from whom are all things and for whom all things exist, you make us participants of the great privilege of procreating children. Your Word establishes that "…therefore a man shall leave his father and mother and be joined to his wife and the two shall become one flesh." You blessed the marriage and gave the mandate to: "Be fruitful, and multiply, and fill the earth and subdue it." This mandate resonates in our being. Our heart's desire is to conceive a baby. The word conceive implies to imagine, to create, to admit, to express, to discern, and by faith, we believe that at the appointed time you will visit us; and according to our time in life, we will conceive a baby.

As a couple, we enter into an alliance with you to take part in the wonderful gift of giving life. We recognize that without you we can do nothing. For this reason, we present our bodies to you as a temple and living sacrifice, holy and pleasing to you, for this is our rational way to worship you. May you, in your great love and faithfulness, prepare our bodies to conceive a baby. Forgive us for the times we have submitted our bodies to sin. We renounce everything that could have withered or harmed our bodies and impede procreation. Free our physical bodies from all generational curses, iniquity, congenital or acquired illness. Wash us with the blood of Jesus. "Create in us,

Oh God, a clean heart and renew a steadfast spirit within us." We ask you, with all our hearts, to prepare our spirits, souls and bodies to be fruitful and conceive. Sanctify and bless our bodies with fertility in order to fulfill your mandate to procreate children.

In the name of Jesus, we claim your promise that there will be no barren male or female among your people because we are a people blessed by you. Sterility, hormonal disorder, low sperm count, lack of ovulation or any other disorders are not part of our inheritance. We declare God's blessings are upon us and that we possess fertile bodies, capable of conceiving children.

We believe our Creator has prepared a table before us in the presence of our enemies. He has anointed our heads with oil; our cup overflows. We trust that if for any reason our bodies have been affected by some physical or spiritual condition, the Creator of our bodies is powerful to do far more abundant work within us than what we can ask or imagine, according to the power that is working in us. We believe that just as God remembered Rachel, opened her womb and gave her children, we will also conceive children for the kingdom.

Convinced of this, we pray that as you preserved the life of the Messiah, while he was in Mary's womb, you will build a protective wall around the ovum, the sperm, and the womb that will receive them, so the power of darkness will not be able to impede your mandate to procreate from becoming a reality. You are the God Creator who has given the order that we be fertile and multiply and have even said that kings will descend from our bowels. Since children are a gift and a reward from you, the LORD, we believe you have prepared a special portion of generational blessing for our baby, so that from its mother's womb he will be a threat to the kingdom of darkness. Allow his mother's womb to be a sanctuary of your peace, surrounded by your virtue, love, compassion and protection. May it be like a fortified city where you have built walls and towers to protect our baby. In the name of Jesus, we pray and thank you. Amen!

Week 2: Preconception: A time of joy and waiting for the moment of Conception.

Hi, it's me again; the baby that already exists in your hearts. I told you I was very smart and I really am; but, I'm not omniscient. Therefore, no matter how much I would like to tell you when my conception will occur in the physical world, I cannot. I may arrive sooner than you think or it may take a while longer. No matter what, think of me as a request that is so, so, special that the Most High God continues to work on me. I suggest that you both make good use of this time and enjoy it; because, I assure you that after I arrive I will take up all of your time; and, you'll miss those days of sleeping until noon.

Since I have already started handing out advice, here's a few more. It's possible that if my arrival is delayed, feelings of disappointment may begin to appear. Don't allow it! Consider each menstrual cycle as a new opportunity for me to be conceived. You can be sure that God will fulfill the desire of those who fear him. He will hear their cry and rescue them. Enter into an agreement with the Most High God to be partakers in his mandate to be fertile and multiply. Believing that although, for now, I'm only a vision, at the appointed moment, time will quickly reach its end and you will not be disappointed. Although my coming may be delayed, you should wait for my arrival because I will surely come.

Oh my loving parents don't despair. God knows well what he is doing. His thoughts and ways are not like ours; for as the heavens are higher than the earth, so are his ways higher than our ways and our thoughts. He has said: "Ask and it will be given to you, seek and you will find; knock and it will be opened to you, for everyone who asks receives, and he who seeks finds, and to him who knocks it will be opened. For who is there among you that if his son asks for bread will give him a rock, or if his son asks for a fish, gives him a snake instead? If you then, being evil, know how to give good gifts to your children, how much more will your heavenly Father who is in heaven give what is good to those who ask him!"

As I've said before, I'm very smart and I like to hand out advice; so, here is another one: You must remain focused until the arrival of the great third week, where your petition will have been answered and conception becomes a beautiful reality. For the moment, although pregnancy has not occurred, everything is ready.

Allow me to give you another short lesson on biology. Once the ovum leaves Mommy's ovary and journeys down the fallopian tube, it is ready to be fertilized. In anticipation of conception, Mommy's body prepares itself for the possibility of a pregnancy. During a 12-24 hour period, as the ovum travels, ready to be fertilized by Daddy, the walls of the uterus prepare themselves to receive the fertilized ovum. If the ovum is not fertilized, the uterus eliminates the walls it has formed (this is called menstruation) to prepare Mommy's body for the next ovum and a new opportunity for pregnancy to occur.

Continue presenting your bodies before God until the arrival of that glorious third week. Don't despair. Be of a steadfast mind, for in God you have a place of safety forever. Remember, God will guard and keep in constant peace those whose mind is inclined toward him. He commits himself to those who lean on him and whose hope and confidence is in him. The Most High God has made everything appropriate in its time; therefore, it is time to remain attached to the true vine. Cry out to the God who favors you. Speak to your soul and ask: "Why are you in despair, oh my soul, and why are you disturbed within me? Wait upon God, for I shall again praise Him, the help of my countenance and my God, my soul waits in silence for God, only because my hope is in Him." Therefore, beloved parents as you wait for my arrival, try with diligence to be found in peace by him, spotless and blameless until the moment of my conception.

The Couple Continues Praying With The Scriptures To Procreate A Baby.

Beloved Most High God, we are confident of this: "He who began a good work in us will perfect it until the day of Christ Jesus." Your Word establishes that those who believe will be blessed, because the things spoken by the LORD will be fulfilled. Therefore, we decree that as Isaac did not allow his father's sterility to become the norm, but took the initiative of praying for his wife; likewise, we claim your promises and blessings so descendants will emerge from our bowels. We surrender our bodies, souls, and spirits to your power, so you may decree in our favor. For if the LORD is for us, who can be against us? Your Word establishes that there will be no woman who aborts or is sterile in your land. Therefore, we believe there will be no physical, generational or spiritual circumstance that would impede the procreation of our baby.

We believe the same power that raised Jesus from the dead will be released upon our bodies. Just as gold is mysteriously formed in the depths of the earth, you will separate and bless us with all kinds of blessings; the ovum and the sperm will embrace each other and give life to our baby. Deposit in them gifts, talents, beauty, wisdom and profound mysteries, so when they come together to give life to our baby, our child will be a priceless jewel, woven by the hands of the most high God.

We know you are a loving God, great in mercy, you know all things and nothing is hidden from you. You yourself have asked us if there is anything too difficult for God. Therefore, we have deposited our trust in you; we will not faint, nor shall we be afraid to receive bad news. Our hearts will be so confident that each menstruation period will be seen as a new opportunity to conceive a baby. We are convinced that you make everything beautiful in its time; and, that our thoughts are not like your thoughts, neither are our ways like yours. We acknowledge that the flesh is weak and sometimes yields to temptation. We ask you to sustain us with your righteous right hand as we wait upon you. Beloved God, we pray that when disbelief tries to take hold of our thoughts, you would give us strength to take every thought captive into the obedience of Christ and order them to wait upon you, for you are our hope, the Most High God who favors us. Help us to be diligent in your peace, believing with all our heart that you are God and you will bless us with blessings from heaven above, with blessings from the deep that lay below and blessings of the breast and the womb.

Finally, we ask you LORD to put a guard over our mouth and to keep watch over the door of our lips so they may only proclaim what is the extraordinary greatness of your power toward us who believe, according to the efficacy of your mighty power. In the name of Jesus, we pray. Amen!

Week 3: I am alive and I describe my development. I measure approximately 1/25 of an inch (0.10 cm).

Something marvelous has happened; I have been conceived! I'm no longer a thought. The hands of the Potter have carefully selected one of Daddy's 500 million spermatozoids to unite it with one particular ovum among Mommy's 120,000 ova.

Although you may not know I exist, the truth is that I'm a marvelous living being, gifted with particular characteristics so as to fulfill an eternal purpose in God's kingdom. The Potter has plans for me and has gifted me with the necessary genes to fulfill his purpose in me.

When Daddy's seed penetrated Mommy's ovum, a group of 46 chromosomes with information coming from each of you embraced and gave me life. My sex was determined at the precise moment of conception by my father's seed; but, it's still a secret for everyone, except for the great Potter.

As I float through the fallopian tube on the way to Mommy's uterus to implant myself, I divide and multiply rapidly. Thirty hours after my conception I have divided into two cells, then into four, and later into eight and continue to divide as I travel through the fallopian tube on my way to the uterus. I am the size of a pinhead and doctors call me a zygote; but, the great Potter calls me his masterpiece, his poem.

Prayer Guide for the Physical Development of Our Baby

You are the great Potter, whose works are marvelous. Our souls know it quite well and our hearts shout to you in gratitude for the miracle of the conception of our baby.

We know that light and darkness are the same to you. For this reason, we ask that as our baby journeys through the fallopian tube on its way to the uterus, and cell division is in process, your eyes would sparkle and shine upon our baby, leading its way with your protective light. You are the one that fashions our baby in its mother's womb. We worship you, for in your image you have formed our child.

We thank you because our baby's sex has already been determined, male or female, you created it. We have no doubt about this. Nothing about our baby is hidden from you. He is an original creation that bears your mark. Your artistic hands are taking care of the colorful embroidery that is secretly and majestically being interwoven in the depths of the mystery of conception.

Great Potter, we ask you to take care of each cell division, as well as the formation of the central nervous system. We pray for your beautiful potter's hands to protect our baby from all type of congenital malformation, which might want to take hold of him.

We know all of his days are written in your book; all of his life is before you, even before they exist. How precious, oh God are your thoughts for us! How immense are the sum of them and the peace of knowing that our baby is in your hands! Many are the marvels you have performed, my LORD, my God and many are your plans for us. No one can be compared to you! If we were to proclaim and talk about your wonders, they could not be numbered. If we were to count them, they would outnumber the sand. In the name of Jesus, we pray. Amen!

Prayer Guide for the Soul of Our Baby (emotions – mind – will)

Oh LORD, you are the great Potter. Our baby is being formed by your artistic hands, just like a potter molds the clay in his hands. Dear Potter, we present you with the formation of our baby's heart. We ask for you to, in a supernatural way, plant the seed of your love, fruit of the Spirit, in the fertile ground of our baby's heart. Let your love be a banner and a seal upon his heart and arm. We ask you to mold him, steer his heart toward your love and toward the perseverance of Christ. Tenderly plant your love in his heart, as a mustard seed, which will bloom, and conform his heart to yours.

Oh great Potter, we ask you to give him understanding and wisdom, so he would keep watch over his heart with all diligence, so streams of life would flow and his soul would be as a watered garden that never languishes. We decree a love song with a good theme will bloom in his heart. Our baby will direct his verses to the King, and his tongue will be as the pen of a scribe.

We prophesy he will walk in love, as Christ also loved us and gave himself for us. He will love you with all his heart, with all his soul, and with all his might. He will be an offering and sacrifice to God, like a fragrant aroma. His identity in you will be like that of Elizabeth, who expressed a sincere love to her cousin, Mary, without showing jealousy or envy, or questioning why Mary had been given the honor of carrying the Savior in her womb. In a spontaneous and natural way, she praised Mary and recognized her as blessed among all women.

We declare that our baby belongs to you. We dedicate him to you from his mother's womb. He will walk in the way of wisdom and in upright paths. At the end of his days, you shall say to him: "I know your deeds, your love, your faith, your service and your perseverance, and your latter deeds are greater than your former ones." In the name of Jesus, we pray. Amen!

Prayer Guide for the Spirit of Our Baby

Dear baby, we have prayed for your physical development and for your soul. Now, we are going to pray for the most important part of your whole being, your spirit. Therefore, in the name of Jesus, we call your spirit to attention. Baby, listen with your spirit to what we are going to teach you. The LORD who stretches out the heavens and lays the foundation of the earth is the one who formed your spirit. He created us in his image and likeness to have dominion. After creating us, he looked at us and said that what he had done was good in great manner. You are the creation of God and he delights in you.

Spirit of our baby, you are the very image of God. Listen now to what the Word of God teaches us about the DNA of God: "Again Jesus spoke saying: I am the light of the world, he who follows me will not walk in the darkness, but will have the light of life." Your God is all light. Spirit of our baby, listen now to what the Word of God says about your spirit. "The spirit of man is the lamp of the LORD that searches deep within the heart." The light of God is part of your genetic makeup. You were created in God's image and likeness to have direct communication with him. God longs for you. You are the Potter's masterpiece. You are the one who has the capability to know the thoughts of your soul and have dominion over them.

We, your parents, bless you with the delight of knowing that you are the property of God, created to give him glory, bring joy to his heart and announce the virtues of him who is calling you into his admirable light. Spirit of our baby, we bless you from the womb with the conviction that you have the right to exert a primary rule over the soul and the flesh. Baby, we bless you with the conviction that you are a spiritual being who has a soul and lives in a body.

We bless you with a spirit sensitive to the voice of the Holy Spirit of God and with an early disposition to invite Christ to dwell in you. We prophesy you will be a friend of the Holy Spirit. You shall know him as your Helper and Comforter. The one who will guide you to all truth and will let you know the things that will be. In the name of Jesus, we pray. Amen!

Week 4: I am alive and I describe my development. I am approximately the size of a mustard seed.

The LORD is my shepherd; I shall not want. I'm about the size of a mustard seed and just as the mustard seed, being the smallest of all seeds, grows into a great leafy tree, so will it be with my formation. However, unlike the mustard seed that has to wait to be planted to begin to grow, an enormous amount of changes are taking place inside of me: my height, sex, color of my skin, eyes and hair have already been determined.

As tiny as I am, I am capable of making the long trip to where I will plant myself. I don't travel alone. The LORD, my Shepherd accompanies me; therefore, I shall not want. He will guide me and show me the path of life, so I may be able to accommodate myself in the depths of Mommy's uterus and become rooted in her walls. Once I'm there, my cells will begin to divide into two groups. One group will form the placenta and the other group will form the specialized parts of my body. My brain, spinal cord, heart and other organs will begin to develop. Two other structures will also begin to develop at this time. They are the amnion and the yolk sac. The amnion contains the amniotic fluid which will cover and protect me during my development. The yolk sac will produce blood and help feed me until the placenta can take over this function.

Prayer Guide for the Physical Development of Our Baby

LORD, you are our Shepherd; we shall not want. You will guide the path of our baby toward implantation; for we know that all his ways are familiar to you. Allow each part of his body in development to be like a tree firmly planted near streams of water which yields its fruit in its season, its leaf does not wither and in whatever he does he prospers.

We present you with the cell division and the two groups which will develop, the ones that will form the placenta and the ones which will form the specialized parts of his body. We ask for the formation of these two groups to be under your care; for we have entrusted you with our baby from his mother's womb. May the yolk sac, which will produce blood and help feed him, be covered by the blood of Christ which has the power to cleanse and protect him from all congenital disorders.

We pray that as his brain begins to develop it would be like clay in the potter's hands and for you to be the Potter. Father, we ask you LORD, to call our baby from his mother's bosom and from his mother's bowels to mention his name.

We declare that just as Ezekiel prophesied and while he was prophesying there was a great noise, then a shaking and the bones came together, each bone with its bone, in this way may our baby's spinal cord be formed by your Word. Allow his heart to be healthy with arteries similar to bubbling springs flowing with life.

We believe that as a shepherd tends his flock and in his arms he gathers the lambs and carries them in his bosom and shepherds them gently, you will shepherd the formation of our baby. You will protect his brain, spinal cord, heart and other organs from any congenital malformation. Faithful is the LORD who will strengthen and protect him from the evil one.

We know God has already spoken in favor of our baby and has said: "The beloved of the LORD shall dwell confident near Him, and the LORD shall cover him always, and he shall dwell between his shoulders." In the name of Jesus, we pray. Amen!

Prayer Guide for the Soul of Our Baby (emotions – mind – will)

Beloved Shepherd who shepherds the formation of our baby, we believe that while our baby is being formed and woven in the depths of his mother's womb, you shepherd him, because your works are wonderful and our souls know it very well. We pray that the seed of love you have sown in our baby's heart will take root and by the power of your word, it will be as embroidered thread interwoven over his heart, causing his heartbeats to be heartbeats of love for you.

Allow him to walk with his face inclined toward you. May he confide and depend only on you, the Good Shepherd. We know the wicked are estranged from the womb; and those who speak lies go astray from birth. We decree this is not the case with our baby; but rather, even from the womb the need to seek and inquire of your presence is infused into his soul. He will seek you and find you. For your Word establishes that those who seek you with all their heart and soul will find you.

We prophesy that just as Jonathan loved God and knew to accept his will of establishing a new order, love will reign in the heart of our baby and guide his motives and actions. We believe our baby will love his neighbor as intensely as Jonathan loved David. We declare the favor of God upon our baby. The good Shepherd will guide him through paths of justice; from his childhood he will walk in the paths of God. He will love God and serve him with all his heart and soul. God will be to him like choice gold and silver. Our baby will rejoice in the Good Shepherd. He will raise his face to God to pray; and, God will listen to his prayers. In the name of Jesus, we pray. Amen!

Prayer Guide for the Spirit of Our Baby

Dear baby, we speak directly to your spirit in the name of Jesus Christ. Listen to what the Word of God says about you: "God created man in his own image, in the image of God he created him; male and female he created them." And he adds: "Before I formed you in the womb I knew you and before you were born I consecrated you." You are very special; you were created in the image of the only true God. He has plans for your life. You have been in his thoughts long before being conceived and in his book of life he wrote the precious plans he has for you. They are beautiful plans, higher than the earth, so high that we can't imagine them. So rejoice, for God knows you and right now, while you're in your mother's womb, he is watching over you. He has deposited in you everything you will ever need to achieve God's plan for you.

Listen to what the Word of God says about how he is caring for you. "The LORD is my shepherd; I shall not want. He makes me lie down in green pastures; he leads me beside quiet waters." "He will charge his angels to watch over you and to guard you in all your ways. They will bear you up in their hands that you do not strike your foot against a stone." Dear baby, God loves you and the only thing he asks of you is that you love him with all your strength and with all your being. Let your spirit be tender and serene, like an incorruptible ornament, which is precious before God. Dear baby, we bless you with a steadfast spirit like the Holy Spirit, who doesn't seek recognition. In the name of Jesus, we pray. Amen!

Second Month

Weeks 5-8

Summary of the Pregnancy Process

Week 5:   The development is fast. Practically the entire structure and organs are formed and beginning to function.

Week 6:   Heartbeats have begun. The umbilical cord has developed. The brain grows rapidly.

Week 7:   The baby's face is taking shape.

Week 8:   Cartilage, bone and tongue are beginning to form.

The Prayer Focus Will Be:

Week	Name of God	Bible Character	Prayer Focus The Soul	Prayer Focus The Spirit
5.	Shield	John the Baptist	Fruit of Joy	God's Protection
6.	A Jealous God	Shiprah and Puah	Fruit of Joy	Inheritance in God
7.	LORD of the Heavenly Host	Phillip	Fruit of Joy	Identity in God
8.	The LORD Sanctifies	Simeon	Fruit of Joy	Identity in God

The Festivals of Israel and Pregnancy

The Festivals of Israel	Pregnancy
N/A	N/A

Week 5: I am alive and I describe my development. I am the size of an apple seed.

Many things have happened since I was conceived. I have finally arrived at my new little house, the one the LORD, My Shield, has prepared for me. I am the size of an apple seed. Until now, to the human eye I looked like a beautiful mass of cells; however, from this moment on I begin to take a specific shape. My neural tube, which will later form my spinal cord and brain, runs from top to bottom. The lump you see in the middle is my heart. The four chambers of my heart are already functioning and my heart will give its first beats of love during this week, establishing the rhythm for all the days of my life. When Mommy is given an ultrasonic screening, you will hear how my heart beats with love for you and for my LORD, "My shield around me, my glory and the one who lifts my head." My heartbeat will be music to your ears; a sound that I'm sure will be inscribed in your hearts. The umbilical cord, my lifeline, is developing; my kidneys, liver, gastrointestinal system, lungs, as well as my brain, make their appearance. I'm ready to learn the Word of my God. My arms and legs begin to sprout. Pretty soon I'll be able to dance for my LORD.

Prayer Guide for the Physical Development of Our Baby

LORD, we know that although the beginning of our baby is small, his final state will be great. Thank you for being his shield and protector. We ask you to perfect the formation of his neural tube; cover each nerve with your presence. Protect his spinal cord from any congenital malformation. Safeguard his kidneys, liver, gastrointestinal system and cover them with your presence as they develop in the maternal womb. Cover his heart with your shield so the four chambers are protected and pump with strength and vigor to receive the blood from the veins and for the outflow of blood to the arteries. We pray that his heart rhythm will always beat perfectly.

We present to you his umbilical cord, his lifeline. We decree that just as the priests tied their breastplate with a blue cord, so it would not come loose from the ephod, you secure our baby's umbilical cord. We know that the Spirit of our God knows our baby; and the breath of the Almighty, who gives life, will create his lungs. Dear Lord, guard over the formation of his feet, so they will be as those of a deer, capable of escalating high places. Give him well formed arms and legs to allow him to raise his hands in worship and dance in your presence.

You are the shield around him who will free him from the trap of the hunter, from the deadly pestilence that strikes in the shadows, or the destruction that lays waste at noon. You will cover him with your feathers and under your wings he finds refuge from all congenital malformation. Your faithfulness is a shield and wall. Our strength and refuge is in the God we trust. Hallelujah. In the name of Jesus, we pray. Amen!

Prayer Guide for the Soul of Our Baby (emotions – mind – will)

LORD, we know you are the true vine and we are the branches who receive life from you. Your Word establishes that the joy of the LORD is our strength. Without your joy we lose heart due to the cares of our daily living. Therefore, we ask you to be a shield around our baby. Just as John the Baptist leaped with joy in his mother's womb, let the seed of joy, fruit of the Spirit, germinate in our baby's soul and fill him. We ask for your joy to be in our baby and his joy to be perfect, to the extent that when days of sorrow come his heart will remain firm so nothing or no one can rob him of his joy in you. Allow our baby to know his identity in you and make known to him the paths of life. We know the Kingdom of God is neither food nor drink, but justice, peace and joy in the Holy Spirit. Therefore, baby, we bless you with the joy of knowing who you are in Jesus Christ. We bless you with the joy of knowing you were carefully chosen to fulfill a purpose and the LORD has gifted you with everything you will need to complete it. In the name of Jesus, we pray. Amen!

Prayer Guide for the Spirit of Our Baby

Spirit of our baby, we speak to you in the name of Jesus Christ. Listen carefully to each word we speak; we want to nourish you with the Word of God as the umbilical cord nourishes your physical body. Our desire is that from conception you would abide under the warmth of the powerful Word of God, with the certainty that he who abides in the shelter of the Most High will dwell in the shadow of The Almighty. Baby, God's shadow is like a shield that protected and also guided the people of Israel through the desert. In your life, there will be times when you will walk through the desert. For this reason, we are instructing you in his Word so when these times come your spirit will assume leadership over your soul; and, you will be able to exclaim that your God is a shield to all who take refuge in him. We know that like the nation of Israel, you will not only need a safe haven, but your human spirit will also need to be fed with manna from heaven.

Baby, listen carefully with your spirit to what the Word says about the bread of life God has provided for you: "Jesus said to them: I am the bread of life, he who comes to me will never hunger, and he who believes in me will never be thirsty." With the power to bless and with the spiritual authority God has given to us over you, we bless you spirit of our baby, with hunger and thirst for the Word of God and with open spiritual ears to hear him. In the name of Jesus, we declare, that from the womb your spirit is being quickened and as God instructed John the Baptist, you are being instructed, and even in your days in the desert, you will joyfully announce the wonders of God, who is your Shield and Protector. In the name of Jesus, we pray. Amen!

**Week 6: I am alive and I describe my development.
I measure approximately 1/4 of an inch
(0.64 cm) long.**

My first heartbeats have begun and they are for the God who jealously loves me. My heart belongs to the God who jealously sustains his creation. This week I am growing very rapidly. My umbilical cord has developed. My eyes, nose and ears begin to form, as well as an opening that will be my mouth. My heart has begun to pump blood and most of my other organs are also developing. The buds that have appeared on the sides of my body will become my arms and legs. My brain is growing rapidly. Over the course of the remaining months my brain will develop over 100 billion neurons. I am a genius! The lens of my eyes have appeared, my nostrils are formed and soon the nerves that run from my nose to the brain will appear. My nose moves to its proper place. My pancreas is now equipped to deal with digestive enzymes and the insulin my body needs to function properly. My intestines are growing. Initially, they are located outside of my body, close to my umbilical cord. What a horror! Glory to God, he who watches jealously over me has already made provision to put everything in its place before I am born. Can you imagine trying to carry me around with all my intestines hanging out? And don't even try to imagine how you would change my diaper.

Prayer Guide for the Physical Development of Our Baby

Dear LORD, thank you for so jealously loving our baby. We recognize it was your hands that jealously designed and molded him. What a wonder that in just six short weeks our baby's heart has started beating. Amazing are your works; they surpass anything that can ever be conceived by man. We ask that in the initial formation of his heart, your hands be placed jealously over it. Give him a healthy heart all the days of his life, capable of pumping blood throughout his body to cleanse and nourish it, just as the blood of Jesus cleanses us in the spiritual world. Allow the development of his umbilical cord to be free from any twisting, make it strong, like a three-corded thread, which is not easily broken.

Father, your Word establishes that you look inside the womb and see the growing embryo. Focus your eyes on the development of his eyes and ears; take care of his hearing and allow his vision to be like that of an eagle. LORD, extend your hand and touch his mouth, make it perfect and, even at this early stage, put words in his mouth. We ask you to sanctify his arms and feet. Make his feet like those of the deer, firm and able to sustain his entire body, even in the heights and his arms strong and well formed.

Dear Father, take control of the rapid growth of his brain and the over 100 billion neurons that are developing. Sustain his brain with your loving care so each neuron is healthy and able to function perfectly. Take special care of the lenses in his eyes, the nasal cavities and the nerves that run from his nose to the brain, the positioning of his nose and the development of his intestines. We ask for the Holy Spirit to come upon our baby and the power of the Most High to overshadow him and impart life. Protect his pancreas; make it capable of effectively handling digestive enzymes and the insulin the body needs to function properly. Regardless of his physical inheritance, may diabetes be something completely unknown to him. We decree his body will be free of any type of congenital disease or the tendency to develop them. In the name of Jesus, we pray. Amen!

Prayer Guide for the Soul of Our Baby (emotions – mind – will)

Dear Father, we present to you the soul of our baby; we ask for the beat of his heart to be a song of joy. Do not permit his heart to be inclined to vain things. Baby, we bless you with the joy of knowing you were created to be born at this particular time. Your heart was designed to be comforted and encouraged in love, so you will be able to access all the riches that proceed from the assurance of understanding who you are. Baby, we bless you with the joy of knowing you have been blessed with all spiritual blessings in the heavenly places in Christ, as he chose you in him before the foundation of the world for you to be holy and blameless before of him. We decree you are a powerful weapon in the hands of the LORD, who jealously created you. You will have a joyous nature, firmly rooted in the principles of God.

We prophesy your will shall be subject to the will of God. You will have the joy of seeing the enemy's plans of destruction as opportunities of partnering with God to bless others. We bless you with the character of Shiprah and Puah, the midwives who dared to defy the order of Pharaoh and let the sons of the Hebrew women live. We decree you will also know how to defy the trends of this world by living according to the principles of God. In the name of Jesus, we pray. Amen!

Prayer Guide for the Spirit of Our Baby

Beloved Baby, in the name of Jesus, we call your spirit to attention. Listen to what the Word of God says: "Behold, children are a gift of Jehovah; and the fruit of the womb is a reward." Baby, God calls you his inheritance and adds that you are of great esteem. He is watching jealously over you, and wants to have communion with you. God is good and has already blessed you with every spiritual blessing in the heavenly places in Christ. He chose you in him, before the foundation of the world, for you to be holy and blameless before him. In love he predestined you for adoption as his son. Freely and by pure grace he imparted this upon you through Jesus Christ, his beloved son. This is your great inheritance. We, your parents, bless you with the spiritual conviction of knowing the greatness of the inheritance you have received in Jesus Christ and how great is the hope of your calling and the riches of the glory of your inheritance in Jesus Christ. In the name of Jesus, we pray. Amen!

Week 7: I am alive and I describe my development.
I measure approximately 1/2 an inch (1.27 cm).

The LORD of Hosts is with me; my shelter is the God of Jacob. Thanks to him, with only seven weeks (actually they are five) and scarcely about half an inch in length, I'm quite a character. My facial features are now visible. At the end of my arms, my hands have begun to appear, although for now they look like little paddles. Yeah, I know I look like an extraterrestrial being, but that will soon change; for I am a masterpiece in process. The hand of my God has been kind to me; and I am convinced that he who began a good work in me will perfect it. As a matter of fact, the refinement process has already begun and my mouth, nasal passages, eyes and ears are some of the facial features being defined. This week, my hair follicles and my nipples are formed; my knees and elbows become visible. My main muscular system has developed; I can move and kick. If you could see me, you would realize that I can move like a karate expert. Well, perhaps I'm exaggerating. My main organs, like my brain, digestive tract, pancreas and lungs all continue to develop.

My eyes have their retina and lens; yet, I am still unable to see. I have my own blood type. My beautiful baby teeth have begun to develop beneath my gums. During this week, my unbiblical cord is forming, which will supply oxygen, nutrients and allow the elimination of my waste without the use of a diaper.

Prayer Guide for the Physical Development of Our Baby

Our baby is seven weeks old and we praise and thank you; for we know it is you who give him life. He shall not perish nor be taken from his mother's womb; for as a mighty warrior you will protect him. Oh God of Hosts, we ask you to saturate his physical body with your presence. May our baby be a reflection of your love and beauty. We invoke your Word upon our baby; for it has the power to cleanse. Father, we present his physical features which are being defined. We ask you to apply your chisel and sculpt every detail of his mouth, nasal passages, eyes, ears and face. Allow his arms to be perfectly sculptured by your skilled, artistic hands. Give him firm muscle tone, like marble columns founded on fine-gold bases. Take special care of the formation of his brain, his neural tube and the cellular division taking place. May he have healthy cells capable of communicating with each other and migrate to their destination. Bless his digestive tract and pancreas; we declare they will be healthy. Our baby will not suffer from acid reflux, milk allergy or any other digestive disorder.

Give him powerful lungs, capable of inhaling and exhaling, so he can proclaim to the four winds that you are his LORD. We thank you for his own blood type. We bless him with healthy blood and decree he will not have any type of blood disease. Give him the eyes of an eagle; protect his retina and the lens that cover it. We bless his gums and pray they will be healthy. We bless his teeth, declaring they will be strong, healthy, perfectly aligned and beautiful, like white pearls. In the name of Jesus, we pray. Amen!

Prayer Guide for the Soul of Our Baby (emotions – mind – will)

Oh God of the Heavenly Hosts, we know our baby will face a world filled with turbulence where joy has been substituted for desire, anxiety and depression. For this reason, we ask that from his mother's womb, the seed of joy, fruit of the Holy Spirit, begin to germinate in all his being. Make him loving, joyful in hope and persevering in suffering and capable of bringing your joy to others. Guard his heart and reveal to him his identity in you, the LORD of the Heavenly Hosts, who battles in his favor.

We decree that his trust is only in you; therefore, he will never be confused. May he learn to rejoice in your presence and wait upon you with the conviction that you will grant him the desires of his heart. Do not allow his emotions to be like the waves of the sea that are driven by the wind, but that your principles bring joy to his heart and illuminate the eyes of his understanding. Let him rejoice in obeying your statutes and commandments. May he fulfill them with all his heart, soul and strength, like Philip who taught the scriptures and brought many to salvation. Baby, we prophesy, that as Philip, your spiritual eyes and ears will be open to receive special assignments from God, through beautiful angelical experiences, which you will accomplish with speed, passion and dedication. In the name of Jesus, we pray. Amen!

Prayer Guide for the Spirit of Our Baby

Baby, we want you to listen carefully with your spirit to what the God of the Heavenly Hosts says about you. Therefore, in the name of Jesus Christ, we direct our voices to your spirit to speak to you about the glorious future that awaits you in Christ Jesus. The Word of God says: "For those who are led by the Spirit of God, those are the sons of God." Baby, you have not received a spirit of slavery to live in fear, but have received a spirit of adoption; therefore, you can call God "Daddy." The Holy Spirit will give testimony to your spirit that you are a son of God, and, if son, also an heir, heir of God and fellow heir with Christ. Being a son of God is the inheritance that awaits you in Jesus Christ. We, your parents, bless you with a profound identity in Jesus Christ, with the spiritual conviction that you are much loved by God. You are so loved that he already made provision for your spiritual salvation and your return to him once you have ended your days on this earth. We bless you with a close relationship with your spiritual Daddy. Your encounters with him will be in an atmosphere of intimacy, love and reverence before his greatness. They will cause you to bow down before him and worship him as he desires to be worshipped, in spirit and in truth. In the name of Jesus, Christ we pray. Amen!

Week 8: *I am alive and I describe my development.*
I measure approximately .63 inches (1.6 cm)
long and weigh about 0.04 ounces (1.0 g).

The LORD is the one who sanctifies. What a wonder! While I rest and grow inside my mother, my LORD sanctifies me and separates me for himself. The same way I perceive his care for me, I can already perceive the sounds that come from inside and outside of my personal pool, which is called the amniotic sack. It's time for you to sing to me. Why not write and sing to me my own lullaby? You can also begin to engrave portions of the Bible in my heart and mind. Remember, faith comes by hearing and hearing by the Word of God. What a wonder that God established my hearing to be among the first of my senses to develop. My cartilage and bones have begun to form.

By the end of this week, I will have completed 1/5 of my developmental journey within my Mommy's tummy. I greatly enjoy having a personal pool as my little house. My fingers and toes have appeared but are webbed and short. No gold rings for the moment! I can bend my elbows and wrists. I'm serious about what I said about karate. My eyes are becoming more obvious. They have begun to develop pigment in the retina. My tongue has begun to develop and my intestines are accommodating themselves in my abdomen. Glory to God! I didn't like the idea of having my intestines exposed. The buds that will form my genitals have appeared, but are not sufficiently developed to determine whether I'm a boy or a girl. This continues to be a closely kept secret between myself and my Creator. At the end of this week I end the stage where I'm called an embryo. From now on I'll be called a fetus. Did you know that in the language of the Bible (Hebrew and Greek) the words embryo and fetus do not exist? This is because, for my Creator, I am a living being from the very moment I was conceived. I am His masterpiece.

Prayer Guide for the Physical Development of Our Baby

Beloved heavenly Father, thank you for the gift of hearing. We ask you to care for the hearing of our baby; may the sound of his mother's heartbeat be music to calm him and offer him security. Take care of the formation of his cartilage, which will serve as a support structure and give certain mobility to his joints, as well as covering the bone endings of the joints.

We thank you because your strong hand has been upon our child. Our baby has completed 1/5 of his formation journey. Although his beginning has been small, his end will increase exceedingly. We present you with the formation of his fingers and toes. We ask that as you formed the moon and the stars with your own fingers, you would also form our baby's hands with five fingers and his feet with fives toes on each one. Give him well formed fingers and joints that allow him to flex his elbows and wrists; so together with his arms, he may be trained and capable of breaking a steel bow. We pray that as you guarded Jesus' bones and not one of them was broken, you would guard the bones and joints of our baby.

Watch over his eyes so they may be like those of a dove. Paint them with the color pigment of your choice, but above all, sanctify them. Keep them from being fixed on vain things. Thank you for the formation of his tongue. We pray that from the beginning of its formation you would enable it to carry out its function of helping with chewing, swallowing, perceiving taste and in producing speech. Care for the formation and final settling of his intestines inside his abdomen. Thank you for the sex of our baby, for male or female, you created it. In your hands we trust the formation of the genitals that are just beginning to appear. In the name of Jesus, we pray. Amen!

Prayer Guide for the Soul of Our Baby
(emotions – mind – will)

You are the God that sanctifies us; we have been created for the praise of your glory. Father, we ask you to sanctify the soul of our baby. Give him a joyful heart which would gladden your countenance and sing with joy in the shadow of your wings. May he joyfully sing in the morning about your power and your mercy with the certainty that in the day of anguish you will be his fortification and his refuge.

We bless our baby with the joy of receiving revelations from the Holy Spirit, just like Simeon, who knew that he would not see death without first seeing the Savior. We declare his heart is in the hands of Jehovah, and like streams of water, he lovingly directs it wherever he wishes. We prophesy he will call out to you with his mouth and you will hear him; for he will seek you with all his heart. He will be of firm purpose, kept in perfect peace, because his trust is in you. He will hear the voice of God and will know to trust and wait for the fulfillment of God's promises. In the name of Jesus, we pray. Amen!

Prayer Guide for the Spirit of Our Baby

Baby, as we have been praying for your physical development and for your soul, we are now going to pray for your spirit, which is the most important part of your being. Therefore, in the name of Jesus, we call your spirit to attention. My baby, listen with your spirit to what God tells you: "For God so loved the world, that he gave his only begotten Son, that whosoever believes in him should not perish, but have everlasting life. Because God did not send his Son into the world to judge the world, but that the world might be saved through Him. He that believes in Him is not condemned; but he that does not believe in Him is already condemned."

Baby, God loves you deeply, much more than we could ever love you. He loves you so much that he opened a way for you, through Jesus, to have free access to him. Baby, these things which we speak to your spirit can only be understood by your spirit. They are spiritual truths which need to be discerned spiritually by you with the help of the Holy Spirit, so they can be integrated in your heart and mind. For the moment, we only want to teach you that God jealously longs for you. You are very important to Him. He has given you the capability of having the mind of Christ, to be instructed and to judge all things. You will do this by combining spiritual thoughts with spiritual words with the help of the Holy Spirit. Therefore, we bless you with the blessing of knowing your God, being a friend of the Holy Spirit and with knowledge to instruct multitudes. We prophesy you will have the tongue of a disciple, capable of sustaining the weary with a timely word, and with an ear that, day after day, wakes up attentive to hear the things the Holy Spirit wants to tell you. We bless you in the name of Jesus. Amen!

Third Month

Weeks 9-13

Summary of the Pregnancy Process

Week 9:   The digestive system and internal reproductive organs begin to form. The joints have formed and the fingerprints are imprinted on the skin.

Week 10:   The placenta begins to function during this week or the next. Between week 9 and 10 (at 50 days), doctors refer to the baby as a fetus.

Week 11:   Various organs are formed and begin to function. The fingers and toes are separated and well formed.

Week 12:   The vocal cords begin to form. The intestines continue to accommodate themselves. The liver begins to function and the pancreas begins to produce insulin.

Week 13:   The eyes and ears continue to develop. The hands become more functional. The baby is nourished through the placenta.

The Prayer Focus Will Be:

Week	Name of God	Bible Character	Prayer Focus The Soul	Prayer Focus The Spirit
9.	God Almighty	Abigail	Fruit of Peace	Identity in God
10.	God of All Flesh	Daniel	Fruit of Peace	Identity in God
11.	Adonai	Esther	Fruit of Peace	Identity in God
12.	Faithful and True	Eunice	Fruit of Peace	Spiritual Senses
13.	Jehovah, Shalom	Jael	Fruit of Peace	Spiritual Senses

The Festivals of Israel and Pregnancy

The Festivals of Israel	Pregnancy
Festival of Weeks or Pentecost Lev 23:16: You shall count fifty days to the day after the seventh Sabbath; then you will present a new grain offering to the Lord.	**Development of The Baby** On the 50th day of pregnancy, the doctors no longer refer to the baby as an embryo. They identify him as a fetus. The baby now has the form of a human being.

**Week 9: *I am alive and I describe my development.
I measure approximately 0.9 inches (2.3 cm)
long and weigh about 0.07 ounces (2.0 g).***

Abraham was 99 years old when the Lord appeared to him and said: "I am God Almighty; walk before me, and be blameless." God Almighty is the one who formed me. When he looks at me, he looks at me as he looked upon Moses and saw him beautiful in his eyes. That's the way you should look at me, with the eyes of your heart.

Although the bud at the end of my spinal cord has gotten smaller and almost disappeared, my head is very close to my chest and it's pretty big. I tell you, I look like an alien. Most of my joints are formed; and I like to practice flexing my fingers and feet, as well as grabbing as my ears and nose. Although you may still not be able to feel my subtle movements, I have become quite a dancer as I move from one side to the other in my little house. How I wish I could already wrap my fingers around the fingers of my Mommy and Daddy. Who knows? Perhaps in Mommy's next ultrasound, I'll get a chance to show off how I can flex and grab with my fingers. If you could only see me! The tip of my nose has developed and can be seen in the profile. The loose skin over my eyes has begun to form my eyelids; they will become more noticeable in the next few weeks.

My digestive system continues to develop. My anus is forming and the intestines grow longer. This is a very important week. My internal reproductive organs, such as testicles or ovaries, start to form. Something miraculous has happened! My fingerprints have already been imprinted. My own unique fingerprints, the ones my Creator made just for me, just as the Almighty has inscribed me on the palms of his hands.

Prayer Guide for the Physical Development of Our Baby

Father, we know that you make everything beautiful in your time, that our baby is your workmanship, created in Christ Jesus to do good deeds, which God prepared beforehand, so he may walk in them. We are sure that you, our Almighty God, will take care of every detail of his development. We present you with his spinal cord, responsible for carrying nerve impulses and for the communication between the brain and the rest of his body. We ask your divine protection upon it; give it your divine touch, tune each channel of communication and develop it to perfection.

We speak the Word of God upon our baby and declare it will be medicine to his bones. Bless the movements of our baby; allow our child to have agility and flexibility in its joints and movements. Give form to his nose with your artistic hands, allowing him to have a beautiful nose. Thank you, because you carefully clothe him with skin and with it you covered his eyelids. Oh LORD, you who see the entrails and the heart, look at his whole digestive system as it is developing. Focus your eyes on it and care for its formation so he will enjoy a healthy digestive system all the days of his life, able to eat everything you have created for his nourishment.

We present his internal reproductive organs before you and remind you of your promise that there would be no sterility in the midst of your people. We, therefore, claim this promise upon the ovaries or testicles beginning to develop. Thank you for your originality and for giving him his own fingerprints. In the name of Jesus, we pray. Amen!

Prayer Guide for the Soul of Our Baby (emotions – mind – will)

Almighty LORD, we ask you to plant the seed of peace, fruit of the Holy Spirit, in the heart of our baby, so your peace may sustain him in the midst of a world ruled by uncertainty. May the roots of the seed of peace grow like a three-corded strand that extends toward his mind, his emotions and his will. Allow him to have a passionate peace which, refuses to be governed by his emotions and stands firm on the gospel of peace. We pray he will always strive to preserve the unity of the Spirit in the bond of peace, for blessed are those who seek peace, for they shall be called the sons of God.

We decree that our baby will be like Abigail, a model of diplomacy, prudence and good understanding. May he know when to forgive the foolishness of those who surround him and to appease the anger of those in authority. We prophesy that although the world has tribulation, there will be peace and trust in his heart, convinced that God will not allow him to be tempted beyond what he can endure. In the name of Jesus, we pray. Amen!

Prayer Guide for the Spirit of Our Baby

Baby, we direct our voices to your spirit in the name of Jesus Christ. Listen with your spirit to what the Word of God says: "Only of your fathers was Jehovah pleased to love them, and chose their descendants after them." "For you are a chosen race, a royal priesthood, a holy nation, a people acquired by God to proclaim the virtues of him who called you out of darkness into his admirable light."

Baby, you're coming to the world to be light in the midst of a world that prefers darkness. These things are not easy to comprehend; but the breath of The Almighty will give understanding to your spirit and will help you realize that you were created to shine. Baby, we bless you with an understanding of the heart of God, his Word, and his purpose for your life. We bless you with a profound peace and security in God, so as you grow and mature, the spiritual world will become increasingly perceptive to you.

Baby, we prophesy your spirit will have a vital and continuous encounter with the Holy Spirit of God. With your face unveiled you will observe, as in a mirror, the glory of the LORD as you are being transformed to his own image, from glory to glory, in order to live in a manner worthy of the calling to which you have been called. We bless you in the name of Jesus, Christ. Amen!

Week 10: I am alive and I describe my development. I measure approximately 1.22 inches (3.1 cm) long and weigh about 0.14 ounces (4 g).

Jehovah, the God of All Flesh has protected my development. Now the doctors call me a fetus; but my Creator continues to call me the wonderful work of his hands, his creation. It's time to thank God. The most critical part of my development is over. All my vital organs have been formed and have begun to function together. Congenital abnormalities are unlikely to develop after this week; but do not stop covering me with your prayers. I like it when you sing and read to me from the Bible.

I now enter a period of rapid growth; don't worry, I'll find a way to fit in my little house. What a horror! My head is about half the length of my body. Glory to God, soon the rest of my body will catch up. Interestingly enough, as external changes take place, such as the separation of my fingers and toes and the disappearance of the protuberance of my column, internal changes are also taking place. Tooth buds are forming inside of my mouth, which will grow into teeth. If I am a boy, my testicles begin to produce the male hormone called testosterone. My eyelids are sealed. The iris begins to develop and my eye color is being determined at this point. You may be asking yourself, what color will they be? Mommy, your placenta will begin to function during this week or the next. It will be responsible for nourishing me and removing my waste.

Prayer Guide for the Physical Development of Our Baby

We fear not for the growth of our baby for the God of All Flesh cares for him and molds him. Lord, we thank you for taking care of our baby during the most critical period of his development. Dear God, we ask you to measure the circumference of his head and bring it to a size that is proportional to his body. Thank you for the normal growth of his body and for the disappearance of the protuberance of his column.

We continue to present you with his spinal column. We ask you to make it strong and straight, like the cedars of Lebanon. Take care of the formation of his toes. Give him beautiful feet so when people see them they can exclaim: "how beautiful are your feet in sandals!" and upon seeing his fingers, glorify the Creator because of their beauty.

If it's a boy, we entrust you with the formation of his testicles and the production of testosterone. During this phase of formation, keep his eyelids sealed, care for the iris and perfect the color of his eyes. Thank you for being a shield over the wonder of the placenta, responsible for the nourishment and removal of the waste our baby produces. In the name of Jesus, we pray. Amen!

Prayer Guide for the Soul of Our Baby (emotions – mind – will)

Blessed be Jehovah, Lord of All Flesh, that according to all he promised, not one of his words have failed of all the good promises he has made. LORD, our God, we believe you have sown the seed of peace in our baby's heart. Just as the rain and the snow come down from heaven and do not return there without watering the earth, making it germinate and sprout, so is your word that comes out of our mouth to bless our baby. We prophesy, our baby's heart will be like the good soil that receives the Word, understands it and brings forth abundant fruit.

His heart will be filled with your peace; his mouth will speak wisdom and his tongue righteousness. His heart's meditation will be with understanding. We decree he will be like Daniel, who was firm in all your ways, kept your commandments, your statutes and the precepts you have ordained. He will keep guard over his mouth and watch the door of his lips so his heart will not lean toward evil, nor practice the deeds of the wicked or enjoy their delights. We prophesy, like Daniel, you will show him the way he must walk. You will bless him with an intimate relationship with the Holy Spirit, who will counsel him at night and will give him intelligence in the sciences, interpretation of dreams and excellence in the administration of everything he touches. In the name of Jesus. Amen!

Prayer Guide for the Spirit of Our Baby

Baby, we direct our voices to your spirit in the name of Jesus Christ. Listen carefully to the different things God says about you in His Word: "The Spirit of God created me, and the breath of The Almighty gave me life." "Behold, I belong to God, like you, I too have been formed out of clay." Baby, you were created by God; his breath gave you life. You belong to him. Listen again to what God says about the creation of man: "Then God said: let us make man in our image, according to our likeness; and let him rule over the fish of the sea, over the birds in the sky and over the beasts and over all the earth, and over every animal that creeps over the earth." "And God blessed them and said to them: Be fruitful and multiply, and fill the earth and subdue it, and rule over the fish of the sea and over the birds in the air and over every living thing that moves over the earth."

Baby, listen carefully with your spirit; when God made the expansion between the earth, the sea and the heavens, he said that what he created was good. He said the same thing when he created the luminaries, the vegetation, the sea monsters and everything else before creating man. But on the sixth day, when God created man, two important things occurred that you need to know. First, God blessed man so he would exercise dominion over all of creation. Secondly, he said what he had created was good in a great manner. Did you hear that? The creation of man was good in a great manner and in a great manner it was good that he blessed man to exercise dominion over all the creation. For this reason, we have not ceased to pray for you and to plead that you would be filled with the knowledge of God's will in all wisdom and spiritual comprehension; so you will walk in a manner worthy of the Lord, pleasing him in everything, bearing fruit in every good deed and growing in God's knowledge. In the name of Jesus, we pray. Amen!

Week 11: I am alive and I describe my development. I measure approximately 1.61 inches (4.1 cm) long and weigh about 0.25 ounces (7 g).

Adonai is the LORD who created me. I am a beauty. I no longer look like an alien. I look like a perfect, miniature, human being. I will not be a miniature much longer. I'm growing rapidly; and during the next nine weeks I will grow about six inches. Practically all my framework and organs are formed and begin to function. My feet are well defined; my toes and fingers are separated and well formed. My hair and nails have begun to grow and my kidneys begin to function. The muscles of my intestinal walls begin to practice the contractions that digest food. My genitals take their form and pretty soon you'll be able to know my gender with an ultrasound. Meanwhile, only my Creator and I know if I'm a boy or a girl.

Prayer Guide for the Physical Development of Our Baby

Adonai, because you clothed him with skin and flesh, you knitted him together with bones and nerves and gave him life and mercy, we worship you eternally. Thank you for the formation of his feet, arms and fingers. We prophesy they are perfectly formed, beautiful, strong and skillful. We believe you will care for the formation of each strand of his hair, just as you cared for the hair of the men that were with Paul when they were shipwrecked. Give him abundant, healthy, lustrous and manageable hair. Allow him to have healthy nails, free from disease. Your Word establishes that the life of the flesh is in the blood. Therefore, we ask you to bless his kidneys so they will efficiently purify his blood. Thank you for giving him a healthy digestive system. Allow the walls of the intestines to effectively digest his food.

We acknowledge that you chose our baby's gender; and we anxiously await to know if our baby is a boy or a girl. As to the formation of the genitals, we believe you, the LORD, do not forsake the work of your hands. You care for their formation to insure they fulfill your eternal purpose for your sons to be fruitful and multiply. We believe that in your great mercy you will free our baby of all type of disease and generational curses, which would want to impede that from his loins would come kings and priests. In the name of Jesus, we pray. Amen!

Prayer Guide for the Soul of Our Baby (emotions – mind – will)

Oh Jehovah, our LORD, how glorious is your name in all the earth. We ask you to sustain our baby in peace according to your promise, so he may have life, be secure, continually paying attention to your statutes and love your Word. We know those who love your law have abundant peace and nothing makes them stumble. We ask that from his mother's womb he will be your servant. Give him understanding to comprehend your commandments and love them more than gold, yes, much more than fine gold. May he esteem your precepts above all other things and despise all deceitful ways. Let the exposure to your Word give him light and understanding, so he will open his mouth and sigh because he yearns for your commandments. Affirm his steps in your Word and let no iniquity have dominion over him. Allow his eyes to anticipate the vigils of the night to meditate on your Word. Listen to his voice according to your mercy, quicken him, oh LORD, according to your ordinances. We know all your commandments are true and our baby, as Esther, will come to this world with a divine purpose in life. You will defend, redeem and quicken him according to your Word, so he can abundantly fulfill the purpose for which you created him. In Jesus name we pray. Amen!

Prayer Guide for the Spirit of Our Baby

Spirit of our baby, we speak to you. Listen to us with your spirit, for we want to feed you with the pure milk of the Word, so by it you may grow in salvation and desire it from the very moment you are born. Up to now we have used the Word of God to teach you about your spiritual identity in him, how special you are to God, how he formed you in his image and likeness and blessed you to exercise dominion.

This week, we will begin to speak to you about the spiritual gifts with which you are equipped and need to develop. Baby, listen with your spirit. Your spirit is the breath of God inside of you; we believe that just as the physical body needs the lungs to live, your spirit needs God to become quickened. We bless you with a clear perception of your spiritual nature and a total spiritual dependence on your Creator. We announce to you that your spirit is the lamp of the LORD that searches your innermost being. We bless you with the conviction that the only way to be happy and fulfill the order of having dominion upon the earth is by surrendering your heart to Christ. We bless you with Christ's revelation in you, with all the expression of who he is, of the authority he gives you in heaven and on earth to govern in the spiritual world as well as in the natural world. In the name of Jesus, we pray. Amen!

Week 12: *I am alive and I describe my development.*
I measure approximately 2.13 inches (5.4 cm)
long and weigh about 0.49 ounces (14 g).

My Creator, the faithful and true God, has begun to form my vocal cords. I am eager to sing a new song of worship and praise to Him and for you, my parents, to hear my first shout of life. The beautiful eyes my Creator gave me come closer to one another. In the meantime, you must be wondering what the color of my eyes are and who do I look like. My ears move to the sides of my head. My intestines continue to position themselves. My liver begins to function. This is important because my liver will be in charge of cleansing my blood, storing and providing the nutrients I need. My pancreas has begun to produce insulin.

Prayer Guide for the Physical Development of Our Baby

We lift our voices to remind you that we have consecrated our baby to you, our True and Faithful God. We pray you would remember his name as you did with Isaiah, when you called him from his mother's womb, from the depths of her bowels. Since your Word says that you are partial to no one, we ask you to remember our baby and for your hands to form each one of his organs. Bless his vocal cords and each fold of the elastic tissues that form it. Allow the sound it emits to be as the strings of a harp to worship you and like the roar of many waters when necessary. Care for the positioning of his eyes, his ears and each interlocking nerve in his brain. May they be like roots near abundant water, so they are nourished and function perfectly. As the Psalmist, we say: "you formed his body in his mother's womb."

We believe you are forming his intestines, which will be capable of extracting the nutrients from the food, forming the feces and expelling them without difficulty. Father, look at his liver that is just beginning to function. We prophesy you will perfect it and as long as our baby has the breath of life, his liver will perform its vital function of producing anti-coagulants, cleansing the blood of bacteria and old red blood cells, producing the enzymes that detoxify, the production of bile, storing of vitamins, absorbing nutrients and transforming them to fat or glycogen.

Place a new genetic over his pancreas, one free from diabetes and all type of disease. What a miracle! It's only been 12 weeks and our baby's pancreas has begun to produce insulin, which controls the level of digested or absorbed carbohydrates. Oh Faithful and True God, we believe that just as you remembered Ephraim and your inside was moved to extend mercy to him, you would also be moved by our baby. In the name of Jesus, we pray. Amen!

Prayer Guide for the Soul of Our Baby (emotions – mind – will)

Faithful and True God, we know the Kingdom of God is not food nor drink, but righteousness, peace and joy in the Holy Spirit, and that the mind that dwells on the flesh is dead, but the mind that dwells on the Spirit is life and peace. The calling you have given us is that, as far as it depends on us, we are to be at peace with all men. Therefore, we ask for the seed of peace of the Holy Spirit to blossom in the soul of our baby. May the God of peace reign upon his life and be so real that, when he enters any place, he will have the ability to pursue that which contributes to peace, to mutual edification and to impart your peace to those around him. We pray the circumstances he sees or emotions he feels do not disturb his heart or make him afraid, for the peace you give is not as the world gives.

Like Eunice, whose life influenced her son, may our baby be surrounded by an intense and contagious spirituality that will influence the life of many. Open his mind to understand the scriptures and believe you are the true vine. We plead he will understand that your fruit is better than gold, even pure gold. We know there will be times when you will have to prune him so he may bear more fruit, but the profit of being pruned is better than choice silver. We prophesy he will yearn to walk in the path of righteousness, with the certainty that you love those who love you. In the name of Jesus, we pray. Amen!

Prayer Guide for the Spirit of Our Baby

Spirit of our precious baby, we speak to you in the name of Jesus Christ. Through the Word of God, we are praying over you; we are feeding you with the bread of heaven God has provided for you. Our hearts' desire is for the God of Peace, himself, to sanctify you completely so your inner being, spirit, soul and body are preserved without blame for the coming of our Lord Jesus Christ. We have already prayed for your physical senses and are convinced that just as your physical body does not have to make an effort to be human, neither does your spirit have to make any effort to be spiritual. Now then, as your parents, we have the great responsibility to nurture your spiritual senses, just as we have to care for your physical body and help you develop your physical senses. As a matter of fact, the Word teaches us that the spiritual senses have to be exercised to be able to discern good and evil. At first, they should be fed with spiritual milk; but a time should come when they can digest solid food. The Word of God will help you to exercise your spiritual senses. Listen with your spirit to what the Word says: "All Scripture is given by inspiration of God, and is profitable for doctrine, for reproof, for correction, for instruction in righteousness, that the man of God may be perfect, thoroughly furnished unto all good works."

In the name of Jesus, we prophesy that the Word of God, which you have heard in your mother's womb, is being engraved in your spirit. We bless you, confident that the Word of God is like the rain and snow that waters the earth, causing it to germinate and sprout, bearing seed to the sower and bread to him who eats. It shall not return void without accomplishing the desire and purpose for which it was sent. In the name of Jesus, we pray. Amen!

Week 13: I am alive and I describe my development. I measure approximately 2.91 inches (7.4 cm) long and weigh about 0.81 ounces (23.0 g).

The LORD is my peace. I have discovered how to inhale and exhale. It's a wonder how I can do this surrounded by Mommy's amniotic fluid. My eyes and ears continue to develop. My neck keeps growing. My hands are becoming more functional. Sometimes, I have fun playing with my fist. All my nourishment is received from my Mommy's placenta. My heart beats twice as fast as Mommy's because the beats of my heart are first for my God and then for you, my beloved parents. It is possible that you will be able to hear them on your next visit to the doctor.

Prayer Guide for the Physical Development of Our Baby

You are Jehovah Shalom, our peace; therefore, our heart shall not be disturbed. Our baby belongs to you and you have taken care of his formation. We know the Spirit of God made our baby; and the inspiration of the Almighty gave him life, taking care of the process of inhaling and exhaling. As you care for the development of his eyes and ears, secretly inscribe your Word in them. Allow his ears to perceive your whispers and your Word to illuminate his eyes. Make his neck like the tower of David, built to exhibit the shields of mighty men. Train his developing hands, as in ancient times hands were trained to effectively handle a sword. Train our baby's hands to fulfill your purpose in his life.

Thank you, Father, for we can rest assured you have surrounded the placenta, from where our baby receives all his nourishment, with your kindness as a shield. We ask you to seduce his heart. May the first movements of his hands be to bring them to his lips to blow kisses of love to you. In the name of Jesus, we pray. Amen!

Prayer Guide for the Soul of Our Baby (emotions – mind – will)

Shalom, Shalom, you are the LORD of peace. God of Peace, we ask you to concede peace to our baby in all the areas of his life so he may have the ability to take your peace to those who lack it. May he have the certainty that his God is the God of Peace, not of confusion and soon he will crush Satan under his feet. We prophesy that just as Jael was used by God to deliver judgment against the life of Sisera, the cruel oppressor of Israel, our baby will be used by God to deliver judgment against the enemy.

We decree that although a host encamp against our baby, his heart will not fear; though war may arise against him, he will be confident. His emotions will not be guided by the impulses of the soul but by the zeal of God and the leading of the Holy Spirit. We believe our baby will reside in your house all the days of his life to witness your beauty and to meditate in your temple. His life will be more radiant than the midday sun and even darkness will be like the morning to him. When he looks around him, he will know that there is hope in God. He will rest assured, without anything or anyone making him afraid and many will ask for his favor. Jehovah Shalom, our peace, in the name of Jesus, we ask that you sanctify our baby in all his inner being. May his spirit, soul and body be preserved without blame for the coming of our Lord Jesus Christ. In the name of Jesus, we pray. Amen!

Prayer Guide for the Spirit of Our Baby

Beloved baby, in the name of Jesus Christ we call your spirit to attention, for from your mother's womb, we want to help you exercise your spiritual senses. We wish to instruct you in God's way, so from infancy you will know the Holy Scriptures, which are able to give you the wisdom that leads to salvation by faith in Christ Jesus.

Baby, listen with your spirit to the powerful Word of God. All Scripture is inspired by God and useful for teaching, for reproof, for correction, to instruct in righteousness, and to cause the man of God to be adequately equipped for every good deed. We decree that the Word of God is instructing you. You will persist in the things you learned while you were in your mother's womb; you will become a man or a woman completely prepared to fulfill your purpose in God. We prophesy, in God's time, your spiritual eyes will open to see the specific role he has given you, so you can commit to it. He will teach you for your benefit, guide you in the way you should walk. He will lead you to preach the Word with great passion in season and out of season. Your preaching will be useful for teaching, for reproof, for correction and to exhort in righteousness with great patience. In the name of Jesus, we pray. Amen.

Fourth Month

Weeks 14-17

Summary of the Pregnancy Process

Week 14: The thyroid gland begins to produce hormones. If it's a boy, the prostate gland begins to develop. If it's a girl, the ovaries move from the abdomen to the pelvis.

Week15: The bones are stronger. The skin is covered with lanugo. The hair has begun to grow.

Week 16: The genitals are sufficiently developed to determine the gender.

Week 17: If it's a boy, the prostate gland and penis continue to develop. Cartilage begins to be transformed into bones.

The Prayer Focus Will Be:

Week	Name of God	Bible Character	Prayer Focus The Soul	Prayer Focus The Spirit
14.	The Lord God	Noah	Fruit of Patience	Spiritual Ears
15.	Eternal God	Job	Fruit of Patience	Spiritual Ears
16.	Faithful and True	Hannah	Fruit of Patience	Spiritual Ears
17.	Creator	Zachariah	Fruit of Patience	Intimacy with God

The Festivals of Israel and Pregnancy

The Festivals of Israel	Pregnancy
N/A	N/A

Week 14: I am alive and I describe my development. I measure approximately 3.42 inches (8.7 cm) long and weigh about 1.52 ounces (43 g).

Just as the Lord God made the heavens and the earth, he has made my thyroid gland to mature and start producing hormones. Male or female, my Lord God created me. If I'm a boy, my prostate gland starts to develop. If I'm a girl, my ovaries will move from the abdomen to the pelvis. It's possible I may know how to suck my thumb. I tell you, I'm every bit of a genius. My bones are getting harder and stronger every day. My skin is covered by a fine layer of fuzz called lanugo. It is the creative way my God invented to protect my skin while I float inside of my little house in my Mommy's tummy.

Prayer Guide for the Physical Development of Our Baby

Oh Lord God, focus your eyes on the thyroid gland of our baby, responsible for regulating the metabolism of his body. Allow your power to cover it with your shadow in order to free it of all type of hormonal disease. We ask you to be LORD over our baby's reproductive organs. Protect them during this stage of development and sanctify them; for our baby belongs to you.

We prophesy that the physical body of our baby belongs to you; it will be the temple of the Holy Spirit. Our child will guard its body from fornication and all sexual sin. LORD, only you know the path of the wind and how bones are formed in a pregnant woman's womb. We depend on your dominion for the protection of the formation and strengthening of our baby's bones. We prophesy that because of your dominion, he will have strong and healthy bones from his conception to his old age.

LORD, we thank you for the lanugo that covers and protects his skin. We ask you to give him healthy and radiant skin. While in the womb, may he have encounters with you that would cause his flesh to radiate, just like Moses' radiated after talking with you. In the name of Jesus, we pray. Amen!

Prayer Guide for the Soul of Our Baby
(emotions – mind – will)

Lord God, our prayer is that the eyes of the heart of our baby be illuminated. May he know what is the hope of his calling, what are the riches of the glory of his inheritance in you, and the extraordinary greatness of your power to us who believe, conformed to the effectiveness of the strength of your power.

We ask that the seed of patience give abundant fruit; so by means of patience and the encouragement of the scriptures, he may have hope in you, the God of patience and comfort. Lead our child to live a life of integrity and righteousness, as your servant Noah did, in the midst of a world very much like ours, where man has corrupted his way upon the earth and violence reigns. Help him to keep from conforming to his surroundings. May he have a renewed understanding of his mind, and regard himself as a living sacrifice, holy and pleasing to you, so after doing your will, he will reap the enjoyment of your promises.

Let him quietly know how to trust and wait with patience and not be upset by the prosperity of the wicked and their intrigue. We prophesy he will put aside anger, abandon violence and not lean toward doing evil, knowing that the evil-doers will be exterminated, for those who wait on the Lord will inherit the earth. Lord God, allow our baby to find favor in your eyes; may his life be like Noah who accepted your calling of building an ark and patiently worked for 120 years without losing his focus. In the name of Jesus, we pray. Amen!

Prayer Guide for the Spirit of Our Baby

Spirit of our baby, we speak to you in the name of Jesus Christ. Listen to what the Word of God says: "My sheep hear my voice, and

I know them, and they follow me." God has determined that his sons will be able to hear him. What a wonderful God is this who allows us to hear his voice and follow him! The Word of God has a lot to say about hearing; as a matter of fact, he establishes that: "Faith comes from hearing, and hearing, by the Word of God."

Your spiritual ears are very important. While you are in your mother's womb, we shall be reading the Word of God to you and talking to you about him. We believe his Word is being planted in your heart. You will not only be a hearer of the Word but personally get to know the God of your fathers, surrender your heart to him and live for him. In the name of Jesus, we bless you with love for the Word of God and a burning desire to hear his voice. We declare you will know how to hear the voice of God and wait in silence to hear his counsel. What you hear will bring conviction to your heart and provoke you to raise your voice to God and say: "Oh Lord, it is you who made the heavens and the earth, the sea and all that is in them, and I will serve only you." In the name of Jesus, we pray. Amen!

Week 15: I am alive and I describe my growth. I measure approximately 3.98 inches (10.1 cm) long and weigh about 2.47 ounces (70.0 g).

The Eternal God continues to care for me. My legs have grown and are longer than my arms. My body is now larger than my head. You will be happy to know that I am constantly moving my hands and feet. Perhaps, you'll feel some fluttering movements in your tummy. It's me! My bones are stronger and I can kick, turn, twist and bend, and all this without karate lessons. If you still can't feel my movements, don't worry; I don't intend to stop moving. I'm pretty sure the day will come when you'll ask me to stop moving!

I can also smile, frown, make funny faces, grab and even suck my thumb. Aren't you impressed with all the things I can do? My skin is still very thin; and, my blood vessels are visible.

The three tiny bones of my middle ear have begun to harden. The auditory centers of my brain haven't developed yet. Perhaps that is why I still can't clearly distinguish what I hear; but my ability to hear is developing. I already have eyebrows and even my hair is beginning to grow. I imagine you are asking yourselves what color hair I will have.

Prayer Guide for the Physical Growth of Our Baby

Oh, Eternal God, thank you for caring for the growth of our baby and the proportions of each part of his body. It amazes us how, being so small, you have given him the ability to move with all his strength. We wait with great expectation for the moment when we will experience the pleasure of feeling his movements for the first time.

Thank you, Eternal God, for giving him the ability to smile, frown, make funny faces, grab and even suck his thumb. We believe, that from the womb, you will fill his mouth with laughter and his lips with shouts of joy. Thank you for covering him with skin. We declare his skin is healthy and will continue to change until it reaches the right thickness. We prophesy his bones will be as strong as steel and his limbs like iron bars.

Eternal God, your Word establishes that your sheep hear your voice, know your voice and follow you. The desire of our hearts is for our baby to know you from his mother's womb. We ask for your creative shadow to cover the developing auditory center in his brain and engrave your voice in it. Look at the initial growth of his hair and allow it to be as soft as silk and abundant as clusters of dates. In the name of Jesus, we pray. Amen!

Prayer Guide for the Soul of Our Baby (emotions – mind – will)

Eternal God, you are our refuge and your eternal arms sustain our baby. Eternal God, your Word establishes that: "Better is the end of the business than its beginning; better is the perseverance of the spirit than the arrogance of the spirit." Therefore, we pray for the fruit of patience to blossom in our baby's soul. We know the steps of a man are arranged by Jehovah and he approves his way. "When man falls, he will not stay prostrated, because Jehovah sustains his hand." Eternal God, we believe that just as Job was able to wait upon you during his years of immense tribulation and you guided his steps, you will also watch over our baby's walk and establish his steps. May the seed of patience yield its fruit and cause our baby to know how to wait upon you with the conviction that you are watching his walk and establishing his steps. We prophesy that guided by your hand, the tribulations that touch his life will yield patience, and patience proven character, and proven character hope, and hope does not disappoint because the love of God has been poured out into his heart through the Holy Spirit that was given to him. In the name of Jesus, we pray. Amen!

Prayer Guide for the Spirit of Our Baby

Our much beloved baby, in the name of Jesus Christ, we now speak to your spirit. Listen carefully with your spirit to what the Word of God says: "He who dwells in the shelter of the Most High shall abide in the shadow of the Almighty." Baby, through our payers to God we have tried to make your mother's womb a sanctuary, so you can develop under the shadow of God. Through prayer, we want to shelter and prepare you to face the world. This portion of the Word of God describes the world in which you'll come to live in: "Son of man, you live in the midst of the rebellious house, who have eyes to see but do not see, ears to hear but do not hear; for they are a rebellious house."

Baby, we decree that you will not abide by the customs of this world. The light of God shines upon you; you understand that it is better to listen to the rebuke of the wise than to listen to the song of fools. Your ears will be closed to the foolish words of the world, and on the contrary, in the morning you will hear God's loving kindness. Your trust will be in him and from your mouth will come this cry: "Teach me, Oh God, the way in which I should walk; to you I lift up my soul. Deliver me, Oh Lord, from my enemies; I take refuge in you. Teach me to do your will, for you are my God; let your good Spirit lead me to solid ground." In the name of Jesus Christ, we declare this. Amen!

Week 16: I am alive and I describe my development. I measure approximately 4.57 inches (11.6 cm) long and weigh about 3.53 ounces (100 g).

Until now, the probability is that Jesus, the Faithful Witness and I are the only ones who know my gender. However, if I do not get shy, perhaps this week you'll discover my gender. My genitals are already well developed and can be distinguish during an ultrasound. It is also possible you may hear the small beat of my heart with an external monitor. My heart already pumps 6 gallons of blood each day and beats twice as fast as Mommy's. I have learned to breathe under water. As I inhale and exhale I help my lungs to develop. Fat is beginning to form underneath my skin, which provides insulation for the coming months. I continue to grow and can proudly hold up my head and neck. I am very much a champion! God is my shield, my glory, the one who lifts up my head! Hallelujah!

Prayer Guide for the Physical Development of Our Baby

Beloved God, Faithful and True, thank you for the sex you have chosen for our baby and for the purpose you have for his life. We present you with his heart, the one you formed. We ask you to give him a strong and healthy heart capable of efficiently pumping his blood with strength. As we pray for him, using your Word, engrave it in his heart.

Thank you for the skin and for the fat that accumulates under it to regulate the temperature of his body. We believe you are his breath of life; therefore, we ask you to strengthen his lungs and prepare them for his life outside of his mother's womb. Thank you for giving him a strong neck, like the tower of David built with rows of stones. We entrust you with the development of his sexual organs. We declare, as the Faithful and True God that you are, that you will faithfully care for their development so they will not have any type of abnormality. From his birth he will identify with the sexual gender with which you created him. In the name of Jesus, we pray. Amen!

Prayer Guide for the Soul of Our Baby (emotions – mind – will)

Faithful and True God, we ask for our baby to know how to patiently wait upon you, as Hannah, Samuel's mother knew how to wait patiently upon you, in spite of Penninah, who provoked and irritated her, annoying and saddening her because she couldn't bear children. Faithful and True God, we ask you to guard his heart and his feet from being seized by impatience. Give our baby a gentle heart that will be life to his body, slow to anger and of great prudence, like Hannah, when she was unjustly judged by the priest.

We bless our baby with the wisdom to wait upon you with the confidence of knowing that in rest he will be safe. He who is steadfast in purpose, you will keep in perfect peace because he trusts in you. Baby, we bless you with a gentle heart which will not reject discipline, nor loathe the reproof of a Faithful and True God, but comprehend that he whom the Lord loves, he reproves as a father the son in whom he delights. Oh Faithful and True God, we ask that our child know how to patiently wait upon you with a willing heart. In the name of Jesus, we pray. Amen!

Prayer Guide for the Spirit of Our Baby

Baby, we call your spirit to attention, in the name of Jesus Christ. Listen with your spirit to what the Word of God tells you: "Thus says the Lord, your Redeemer, the Holy One of Israel: I am Jehovah, your God, who teaches you for your benefit, who points you in the way you must follow." Baby, our hope is that each word we have prayed over you will be planted in your heart and bear fruit. So from your childhood, you will declare what you have heard.

May God reveal to you his hidden and unknown things. May you rise up as his trumpet in the midst of a world where darkness reigns to announce Jesus Christ, the Faithful Witness, the first born of the dead and the sovereign of the kings of the earth. He who loves us and liberated us from our sins with his blood has also made us kings and priests for his God and Father. To him be the glory and dominion forever and ever.

Baby, in the name of Jesus, we declare God is the one who teaches you for your benefit and leads you in the way you must follow. We prophesy your heart will receive and your mind will comprehend the scriptures we have prayed over you. May this instruction produce a renewed mind, which will not conform to this world, so you will experience the knowledge of the good, acceptable and pleasing, complete purpose of God for your life. In the name of Jesus, we pray. Amen!

Week 17: I am alive and I describe my development. I measure approximately 5.12 inches (13 cm) long and weigh about 4.94 ounces (140 g).

As the clay in the hands of the potter, I have been molded by my Creator. My limbs are in proportion to my body; I have the appearance of a baby. Pads are forming on my fingertips and toes. The cartilage of my skeleton is turning into bones. My bones remain flexible to facilitate my passage though the birth canal, which will bring me to the loving arms of my parents.

Wonderful are the works of my God! I will worship him from the womb until my hair turns gray. I can hold my head up straight; and, my eyes look straight ahead but still remain firmly closed. If I'm a boy, my prostate and penis continue to develop. My umbilical cord is now thicker and stronger and continues to rush blood and nutrients to help me grow. Prepare those diapers! My intestines are filling up with what appears to be my first poop.

Prayer Guide for the Physical Development of Our Baby

We thank you, beloved Creator for having cared for each part of our baby's body. His body has continued to grow in proportion, giving him the appearance of a male or female baby. If it's a boy, we ask you to protect the formation of his prostate, which is responsible for the production of the seminal fluid that protects and nourishes the spermatozoa contained in the semen.

Beloved Creator may the cartilage of his skeleton, which will turn into bone, be like the green grass in your hands. We exalt you, for we know his body is not concealed from you, although it was made in secret and woven in the deep. Thank you for sustaining his head; for we believe that his neck is like a column of cedar. Let his umbilical cord, his lifeline, be like the cord of scarlet thread that saved the lives of Rahab and her family. Allow it to become strong and supply the necessary nutrients. Keep it from wrapping itself around his neck at the time of birth. In the name of Jesus, we pray. Amen!

Prayer Guide for the Soul of Our Baby (emotions – mind – will)

"Then a shoot will spring from the stem of Jesse, and a branch from his roots will bear fruit." Lord, you are the stem that has given fruit; we ask for the root of patience, fruit of the Holy Spirit, to feed the soul of our baby as it fed Zachariah, the priest, who diligently served you and walked blameless in all your commandments.

Dear LORD, we are aware that our child will be born in an era where people expect everything to happen quickly, very different from the way you tend to operate. For this reason, we ask you to deposit the fruit of patience in his life. Help him understand how you, being Almighty God, took your time in creating the earth, that there is an appointed time for every matter and you have made all things beautiful in your time. We pray for our baby's mind and emotions to embody your patience and character. Give him a teachable heart.

May he not part his eyes from you; incline his ears to your reason, pay attention to your Word and keep it in the midst of his heart. Your words are life to those who find them and health to their whole body. Help him to guard his heart with all diligence, like Zachariah, because from the heart flow the springs of life. May he keep his mouth from perversity and depart from deceitful lips. Let his eyes look straight ahead and his gaze be fixed on the path beneath his feet so his ways may be established. He will not turn to either the right or the left and he will keep his feet from evil. In the name of Jesus, we pray. Amen!

Prayer Guide for the Spirit of Our Baby

Baby, we continue to pray for the most important part of your being, your spirit. Therefore, in the name of Jesus, we call your spirit to attention. Baby, listen with your spirit to what the Word of God teaches us: "As the Father has loved me, I have also loved you; remain in my love, just as I have kept my Father's commandments and remain in His love. These things I have spoken to you so that my joy may be in you and that your joy be complete."

We bless you with a life of spiritual intimacy with God, with a thorough understanding that in everything you have been enriched in him, that is, in all speech and knowledge. Baby, you do not lack any of God's spiritual gifts. You can eagerly await the revelation of these through our Lord Jesus Christ, who will confirm you until the end, for you to be blameless in the day of our Lord Jesus Christ. Faithful is God through whom you were called into communion with his Son, Jesus Christ, our Lord. Baby, we bless you with the spiritual knowledge of the riches of his glory, with being strengthened with the might of his Spirit in your spirit, in order for Christ to dwell in your heart by faith so you will be rooted and grounded in love. May you be able to comprehend with all the saints what is the breath, length, height and depth of his love. Also to know the love of Christ, which surpasses knowledge, so you may be filled with all the fullness of God. In the name of Jesus, we pray. Amen!

Fifth Month

Weeks 18-21

Summary of the Pregnancy Process

Week 18: The lungs continue to form and the vocal cords are formed.

Week 19: The nerves in the body are being coated with a substance that protects them and allows the neurological impulses to flow gently. The reproductive organs continue to develop.

Week 20: The cells for touch, smell, hearing, sight and taste are developing in specific areas of the brain.

Week 21: The white cells which form the defense system are in formation. The tongue is completely formed. If it's a girl, the uterus and vagina are formed.

The Prayer Focus Will Be:

Week	Name of God	Bible Character	Prayer Focus The Soul	Prayer Focus The Spirit
18.	Lord of Heaven	Barnabas	Fruit of Kindness	Identity in God
19.	Banner	Shunammite	Fruit of Kindness	Spiritual Senses
20.	Our Shepherd	John	Fruit of Kindness	Quickened
21.	Our Strength	Ruth	Fruit of Kindness	Strengthened in God

The Festivals of Israel and Pregnancy

The Festivals of Israel	Pregnancy
N/A	N/A

Week 18: I am alive and I describe my development. I measure approximately 5.59 inches (14.2 cm) long and weigh about 6.7 ounces (190 g).

If you could only see me! I weigh almost half a pound! I am beautiful, a masterpiece of the LORD of Heaven. My ears have reached their final position. Yucky, they kind of stick out a little from my head. In the coming weeks the bones of my middle ear and the nerve endings in my brain will be formed. I'll be able to hear Mommy's heart beat and the sound of my blood moving through my umbilical cord. My vocal cords are forming. Although I go through the gesture of crying, since there is no air I don't make a sound. The fact is that I have no reason to cry. The Word of God that has been prayed over me is engraved in my spirit; the love you give me fills all of my being and produces a joy that floods my heart. Parts of my heart, including the ventricles and chambers, should already be visible. The next time Mommy goes for an ultrasound you will get to see how my heart beats with love for you and for my Creator.

My eyes are also forming; for the moment they look straight ahead. It is possible that the retina can detect the beam of a flashlight if you point it toward my little house. My spirit already perceives the light of my Creator.

This week my bones begin to harden or ossify. Did you know that some of the first bones to ossify are the ones that form my clavicle and my legs? Beautiful little pads are beginning to form at the tips of my fingers and toes.

Meconium, my first intestinal waste, is accumulating in my intestines. Relax, the Lord of Heaven took care of this; for the moment you don't have to think about changing diapers. Mommy, if you notice sudden but synchronized movements in your womb, don't worry, it's possible that I have the hiccups.

Prayer Guide for the Physical Development of Our Baby

Lord of Heaven, look after the development of our baby during this week. We ask you to guard the route of the final positioning of his ears. May your divine hands take care of the formation of the bones in his middle ears and the nerve endings for hearing that are forming in his brain.

By your mercy, we ask you to bless his vocal cords. Your Word establishes that from the mouth of children and nursing babies, you established strength, because of your enemies, to silence the enemy and the revengeful. We know our baby will be born with a destiny in you. Therefore, we ask you to guard his vocal cords; may they be healthy and powerful, capable of giving praise to exalt your name and in the presence of gods, sing praises to you.

We believe you, the Lord of Heaven is in the midst of our baby; by your power, you will save him; rejoice over him in love and sing songs of love that will permeate his heart. For, behold, he who forms mountains and creates the wind and declares to man what are his thoughts, he who makes dawn into darkness and treads the high places of the earth, the LORD, God of Hosts is his name. It is to you to whom we entrust the physical formation of our baby's heart. We ask you to give him a pure and healthy heart, capable of receiving blood from his veins and passing it into the ventricles, so it circulates through the arteries without any impediment.

We acknowledge your power over all blindness; for you are the God that opens the eyes of the blind. Therefore, we ask for your protective light to shine upon his retina, the tissue sensitive to light, located in the interior of our baby's eyes. Give him perfect vision, capable of being illuminated by your Word for the rest of his life. Care for the formation of his bones and free him from all deformity or disease of the bones. Cover his intestines, allow them to extract the nutrients from food and to eliminate all waste from his body. We ask you to free him from all intestinal disease. In the name of Jesus, we pray. Amen!

Prayer Guide for the Soul of Our Baby
(emotions – mind – will)

LORD of Heaven, we present you with the soul of our baby. We ask for kindness, fruit of the Holy Spirit, to bloom in his heart and become like a tree firmly planted by a stream of water. Let his heart be full of love, compassion and kindness; and as the result of our teaching produce a love born of a pure heart, a good conscience, a sincere faith and a kind character capable of mercy.

We pray no one will deceive him with empty words, but that the Holy Spirit will always help him examine what pleases you. May he refuse to participate in the unfruitful deeds of darkness, but instead be willing to expose them with the conviction that it is disgraceful even to speak of the things that are done by them in secret. On the contrary, with deeds of kindness he will expose your light.

We decree he will be a son of consolation, like Barnabas, a good person full of faith and of the Holy Spirit. He will be one that examines what pleases God and takes action. He will act as Barnabas did when he presented Paul to the apostles, telling them how Paul had seen and heard the Lord in Damascus and was now boldly speaking in the name of Jesus. Baby, we declare your life will reflect the life of Jesus. We pray, no matter how many people pressure you, you will feel mercy and respond to the need of those who surround you. In the name of Jesus, we pray. Amen!

Prayer Guide for the Spirit of Our Baby

Baby, we direct our voices to your spirit in the name of Jesus Christ. Listen with your spirit to the Word of God: "To this end we also pray for you always, that our God deems you worthy of his calling, and fulfill every purpose of kindness and every deed of faith with his power, so the name of our LORD Jesus Christ be glorified in you and you in Him, by the grace of our God and the LORD Jesus Christ."

We, your parents, have been praying for you with the conviction that the Word of God says: "And all your sons will be taught by Jehovah; and the peace of your sons will be multiplied." Therefore, we bless you with the certainty that by the merits of Jesus Christ, you are worthy of the calling of God upon your life; and he fulfills in you all desire for kindness and the work of faith with power, so the name of Jesus Christ will be glorified in you and you in him, according to the grace of our God and the Lord Jesus Christ. We ask God to give you abundant faith to direct your path and make you grow in love for all those around you. In the name of Jesus, we pray. Amen!

Week 19: I am alive and I describe my development. I measure approximately 6.02 inches (15.3 cm) long and weigh about 8.47 ounces (240 g).

My Lord, My Banner, made me free! Although, I have a bit of Mommy and a bit of Daddy, I already have my own routine for waking, sleeping and even my favorite position for sleeping. Who knows, perhaps it's a little like one of you likes to sleep! I may even like to take up the whole bed; you'll soon find out.

Like beautiful embroidery with different shades of color, the nerves that traverse my body are being coated with a substance that protects them and allows the neurological impulses to flow smoothly. There is hair on my head already. My Creator has counted them and knows how many there are. My permanent teeth begin to form behind my baby teeth. My reproductive organs begin to develop. If I'm a girl, my uterus begins to develop, as well as the vagina and fallopian tubes. If I'm a boy, my genitals can be clearly distinguished. My kidneys already produce urine.

Prayer Guide for the Physical Development for Our Baby

Beloved God, we thank you for being Our Banner. You are the one who fights for us and raises the flag of victory in our favor. We present you with the physical body of our baby and by faith we establish your name, Jehovah Nissi, Our Banner, upon our baby. We declare that you care for our baby. We give you thanks for guarding his rest. Your Word establishes that in peace he will both lie down and sleep, because you alone, Lord, make him to dwell in safety. Father, we ask that from the womb our baby develop a pattern of restful sleep and insomnia will be completely unknown to him.

We declare his nervous system is a beautiful embroidery your artistic hands have formed, majestically interwoven, perfectly covering each nerve, so each impulse will flow to perfection, today and always, just as your love flows toward us. We thank you for the perfect care of our baby; you are even concerned with the number of hair on his head.

Father, we take hold of your promises and affirm that his baby teeth, as well as his permanent teeth, will be perfectly aligned. They will be strong teeth, free of cavities and oral disease, which may cause the loss of his teeth or misalignment.

We know your Word affirms that God created man in his image, in God's image he created them: male and female he created them, and that your daughters will be like a fruitful vine, and there will be no abortion or sterility among your people. We claim this promise upon the reproductive organs of our baby. We trust its reproductive organs will develop to perfection; they will be fruitful, healthy and will be free from all conditions that could cause sterility. We cover his kidneys, which are already producing urine, with the blood of Christ declaring that today and always they will fulfill their function of cleansing and purifying his blood of toxins. In the name of Jesus, we pray. Amen!

Prayer Guide for the Soul of Our Baby (emotions – mind – will)

LORD, you are Our Banner. You are the one who promised never to leave us and have ordered us to come near the throne of grace with confidence to receive mercy and find grace in time of need. With this confidence, we pray for the seed of kindness, fruit of the Holy Spirit, to flourish in our baby's life. Prepare his heart to be good and just, and retain the Word that has been prayed over him from the womb with perseverance. May it yield fruit a hundredfold. Give him a kind heart, like that of the Shunammite woman, who earnestly and meticulously, without expecting anything in return, prepared a room for the prophet, Elisha.

May all the talents you have deposited in him be put at your disposal by virtue of the grace you have given him. Let him not think of himself more highly than he ought to, but think with sound judgment and realize that all he has is by your grace.

We prophesy that from the womb, you, the Lord his God will teach him to his advantage and lead him in the way he should go. You will call him to righteousness. Your hand will uphold him, watch over him and appoint him as a covenant to the people to open the eyes of the blind, free the prisoners from jail, the captive from the dungeon, and those who dwell in darkness. In the name of Jesus, we pray. Amen!

Prayer Guide for the Spirit for Our Baby

Baby, we invoke the name of Jehovah Nissi, Our Banner, over you. In the name of Jesus, we speak to your spirit, our beloved baby. We declare the grace of our Lord Jesus Christ and the communion of the Holy Spirit are upon you and from this tender age your spirit is quickened.

While we pray for you, you are being enriched in all word and knowledge. We bless you with your spiritual senses open so all things that physical eyes have not seen, nor ears have heard, nor have entered the heart of men, which God has prepared for those who love him, be revealed to you through the Spirit. For the Spirit searches all things, even the depths of God.

Baby, we bless you from the womb with a quickened spirit; so you may know the things of God and what God has given you. Spirit of our baby, we bless you with the comprehension that you were created to rule over the soul. We pray you will retain the standard of sound words, which from the womb you have heard from us. Spirit of our baby, we speak to you in the name of Jesus and exhort you to treasure the Holy Scriptures which you are hearing. They will give you the wisdom which leads to salvation through faith in Jesus Christ. Follow righteousness, faith, love and peace with a pure heart. Then you will speak words not taught by human wisdom, but taught by the Holy Spirit, combining spiritual thoughts with spiritual words. In the name of Jesus, we pray. Amen!

Week 20: I am alive and I describe my development. I measure approximately 6.46 inches (16.4 cm) long and weigh about 10.58 ounces (300 g).

Twenty weeks, half of the waiting period has passed. Soon you'll have me in your arms and I will look you straight in the eyes and thank God for having you. From now on I won't grow so rapidly, but this next period is very important. Don't stop praying for me! Mommy, do you know that you are providing me with the immunization cells which will protect me from viruses you have had for up to six months after I'm born? My heart is getting stronger. My body parts are reaching their normal size. Mommy, soon you will feel the strength of my legs or elbows or maybe even both, as I try to accommodate myself. As each week goes by, my little house seems to be getting smaller.

The nerve cells responsible for touch, smell, hearing, vision and taste are developing in specific areas of my brain. If I'm a girl, my uterus already has about six million ova, but at birth I'll have about one million. Please pray for my ova.

I can hear noises outside of my little house. I can hear your voices. Please continue to sing the same lullaby to me; once I leave my little house, I will recognize it and I'm sure it will sooth and calm me.

Let's do an experiment to see if you can feel how my heart beats for both of you. Mommy, lie down on your back, on a flat surface. Locate your heartbeat by feeling the pulse on your neck. Now place the other hand on your belly. It is very possible you'll cry from the emotion of clearly distinguishing our two heartbeats.

Prayer Guide for the Physical Development of Our Baby

The Lord is our Shepherd, we shall not want. Therefore, we know that the good work which you began with the conception of our baby, you will perfect until the day of his birth. Good Shepherd, your Word establishes that you are the one that gives the heart the impulse of life. Therefore, since you have given the impulse of life to our baby's heart, we believe it is strong and healthy, free from any disease. We declare your blood flows through his heart and makes it a perfect muscle. Bless his immune system so it will be a protective barrier that keeps him immune from all disease.

We ask you, Good Shepherd, to be by his side and impart your strength to his legs and elbows. Shepherd the neurological connections responsible for his five senses. Establish them firmly, as if by still waters from where they receive the neurological nutrients necessary to function perfectly. We know for certain you are the one who created the ears and formed the eyes, so how can they not function? Allow our baby's sense of taste to savor all variety of foods and flavors; may his touch be able to perceive and distinguish textures and his sight to be like that of the eagle.

If our baby is a girl, we prophesy her uterus and ovaries will be healthy and receive your promise of being fruitful. Once again, thank you for our baby's hearing; we know that faith comes from hearing and hearing the Word of God has the capacity to give life to the spirit of man. We prophesy your Word is being engraved in his heart. With his mouth he will proclaim the praise of the Lord from the womb until he returns to his Good Shepherd. In the name of Jesus, we pray. Amen!

Prayer Guide for the Soul of Our Baby (emotions – mind – will)

Dear Shepherd, your Word establishes the importance of guarding the heart, since life emanates from it, and a gentle heart is life and strength for the body. We ask you to give our baby a heart according to yours, and for your law to be in his heart so his feet will not slip. Incline his ears to your teachings, his eyes to your righteousness and let your Word be delightful to his taste. Allow your presence to be a fresh fragrance to him.

May he walk a straight path, not turning either to the right or to the left from your precepts. We pray he will fear you and keep your commandments, invoke you with gratitude at all times, praising your deeds with happiness, speaking of your wonders, singing praises and searching for you continuously.

We prophesy that just as you dressed his physical body with flesh, you have also made provision for him to be dressed in spiritual clothes, which renew themselves toward a true knowledge, according to the image of the God who created him. Father, we ask for the seed of kindness, fruit of the Holy Spirit, to flourish in his heart and make him merciful and thankful. May our baby be covered with compassion, kindness, humility, gentleness and patience, just as John, the beloved disciple, so if anyone has anything against him, he forgives them as Christ forgives us. May the peace of Jesus dwell in his heart. In the name of Jesus, we pray. Amen!

Prayer Guide for the Spirit of Our Baby

Spirit of our baby, we speak to you in the name of Jesus Christ. Listen carefully to what the Word of God says about you: "Certainly, there is a spirit in man and the breath of the Almighty gives them understanding." Baby, the Word of God establishes the existence of your spirit and teaches that your understanding of spiritual things depends on him. This is why, in the name of Jesus, we prophesy that even while you are in the womb, the Good Shepherd will breathe upon you and quicken you. May he refine your spiritual senses from your childhood and enable you to discern right from wrong, so you'll be able to know the things of God.

May you love his Word, walk in his commandments, keep his laws and put them into practice. Baby, we your parents bless you with being guided by the Holy Spirit; for the Word of God establishes that our sons will be taught by Jehovah, and the well-being of our sons will be great. We bless you with the certainty that you are greatly loved by our God. He knows every detail of your life. He will equip you and continue transforming you into his image. In the name of Jesus, we pray. Amen!

***Week 21:I am alive and I describe my development.
I measure approximately 10.51 inches (26.7 cm)
long and weigh about 12.7 ounces (360 g).***

You, oh LORD are Our Strength. Mommy, I am sure you will agree that the LORD is my strength. You probably think that I am an acrobat. It's amazing all the movements I can make as I position myself in my little house and continue growing. Did you know that, up to now, my liver and my spleen were responsible for the production of my red blood cells? Now the spaces of my bone marrow have developed sufficiently to also contribute in the formation of red blood cells. In the third quarter, my bone marrow will become the most important center of red blood cell production. It's important that you pray for my bone marrow. The white blood cells that make up my defense system, to protect me from infection, are also forming.

My skin has changed and is no longer translucent; it is now opaque. If I'm a girl, my uterus and vagina have formed. My digestive system is functioning. I swallow amniotic fluid, absorb the water and digest the rest. My routine of waking and sleeping are becoming constant. It is believed that my biological clock harmonizes with the external clock, even before my birth. Mommy, your time for eating, resting, as well as the different intensities of light and noise, all serve as a signal to me while I'm in your womb. You are my model; with your body, you give me the signal as to when it's time to sleep and when it's time to do my acrobatics.

Prayer Guide for the Physical Development of Our Baby

Beloved God, thank you, you are perfect, you are our strength and protector. We declare that your protective hands are upon the bone marrow, the liver, the spleen and on each red and white blood cell of our baby. We prophesy, his defense system is impenetrable. This is why, today, we sing this song over our baby: We have a strong city; he sets up walls and ramparts for security. His bone marrow is moist and his skin is transformed to perfection.

You have already seen his inward parts and they will function perfectly, eliminating all toxins from his body. Your presence will be with our baby and give it rest. Our baby will have a healthy routine. He will enjoy having time to worship you, bless you, to laugh, to work and rest, because all his neurological system will be programmed by you.

If it's a girl, her reproductive system is sanctified in you and free of any disorder; kings and priests will come from her womb. In the name of Jesus, we pray. Amen!

Prayer Guide for the Soul of Our Baby (emotions – mind – will)

LORD, you are our strength; we are leaning upon you believing your eyes are upon our baby to care for him and guide him on the straight path. The desire of our hearts is for you to pour out your love and kindness upon our baby; so as he grows, neither height, nor depth, nor anything else will be able to separate him from the love God, which is in Christ Jesus our LORD.

We pray, by your grace, you would call him from his mother's womb and reveal your Son to him. Allow the fruit of kindness to abound in his life. Form in him a character like Ruth's, who showed a quiet and merciful character to Naomi, her mother in-law; and like her, our baby will get to know you, the only true God.

May his life be transparent without a trace of pride or arrogance, but with love and kindness he would avail himself to serve others. We prophesy no thoughtless words will come out of his mouth, only words that edify. He will speak with psalms, with hymns and spiritual songs. There will always be a song of worship for you in his heart. He will be an imitator of you, capable of destroying speculations and every lofty thing raised up against the knowledge of you, taking every thought captive to your obedience, so he'll never do anything that can grieve your Holy Spirit. In Jesus, name we pray. Amen!

Prayer Guide for the Spirit for Our Baby

Beloved baby, in the name of Jesus Christ, we call your spirit to attention. Listen to what the Word of God says: "Finally, be strong in the Lord and in the strength of His might. Put on the full armor of God, so that you will be able to stand firm against the schemes of the devil. For we wrestle not against flesh and blood, but against the principalities, against powers, against the rulers of the darkness of this world, against spiritual wickedness in the high places." Baby, from your mother's womb, we bless you with being spiritually strengthened in the Lord and in his strength through the powerful Word of God. Listen with your spirit to what the Bible says about the Word of God: "For the Word of God is alive and effective, and sharper than any two-edged sword, piercing as far as the division of soul and spirit, of both joints and marrow, and able to judge the thoughts and intentions of the heart."

Baby, we bless you with being prepared by the Word to be light in midst of a world where people prefer darkness to light, and due to the increase in lawlessness, many people's love has grown cold. You will not be afraid of the power of the darkness. You will give thanks to the Father, who has qualified you to share in the inheritance of the saints in light.

Baby, we bless you with a spirit that is the lamp of the Lord, capable of searching all the innermost parts of your being and guiding your heart toward the light of Christ. We prophesy, although in the world darkness may reign, you will not fear but will arise and shine because the light of the LORD reaches you and the LORD's glory dawns on you. God is light and in him there is no darkness at all. You will have peace, for he reveals mysteries from the darkness and brings the deep darkness into light. In the name of Jesus Christ. Amen!

Sixth Month

Weeks 22-26

Summary of the Pregnancy Process

Week 22:   The eyelids, eyebrows and nails are completely formed. The brain has entered a stage of rapid growth.

Week 23:   The eyes are formed, although the iris still has no pigmentation. The pancreas has started to produce insulin.

Week 24:   The taste buds have begun to form.

Week 25:   The structure of the spine begins to form joints, ligaments and discs. The body's blood vessels are developing.

Week 26:   The spinal column already has 150 joints, 33 discs and some 1,000 ligaments. In the eye, the retina begins to form. Brain activity for hearing and vision begins to be detected.

The Prayer Focus Will Be:

Week	Name of God	Bible Character	Prayer Focus The Soul	Prayer Focus The Spirit
22.	Our Righteousness	Dorcas	Fruit of Goodness	Identity
23.	Gentle Breeze	The Centurion	Fruit of Goodness	Armor
24.	Ancient of Days	Joseph of Arimathea	Fruit of Goodness	Belt of Truth
25.	Rock of Israel	Rahab	Fruit of Goodness	Belt of Truth
26.	Strong Tower	Josiah	Fruit of Goodness	Breastplate of Righteousness

The Festivals of Israel and Pregnancy

The Festivals of Israel	Pregnancy
N/A	N/A

Week 22:I am alive and I describe my development. I measure approximately 10.94 inches (27.8 cm) long and weigh about 15.7 ounces (430 g).

I am the wonderful creation of the LORD, Our Righteousness! With just about the weight of one pound, I can do great things. I can clearly hear your conversations, hear when you read to me, talk to me and sing to me. Studies have found that when I am born I will react, letting you know I can recognize the book, the song or prayers you repeatedly read, sang or prayed, while I was in my Mommy's tummy.

My eyelids, eyebrows and nails are completely formed. My brain has entered a stage of rapid growth, providing all the necessary cells for my development. The senses I'll use to learn about the world around me are forming day by day. I will probably be a genius. Well, at least for you, I know that I'll be the most intelligent baby that ever existed.

Mommy, with your help, my liver has begun to break down the bilirubin, a substance produced by the red blood cells. If I am a male, my testicles begin to descend to the scrotum, spermatozoa are formed and I am producing testosterone.

The taste buds have begun to develop on my tongue; soon I'll be able to perceive some of the flavors of the food Mommy eats. The nerve terminals and my brain have developed enough for me to feel when I caress my face. How I long to feel my Mommy's and Daddy's hands caressing me as they cuddle me in their arms!

Prayer Guide for the Physical Development of Our Baby

Oh Jehovah, Our Righteousness, we know our baby dwells securely in his mother's womb. Our hearts rejoice and our souls cry out loud, hear me islands and listen distant lands, the LORD has not only awakened our baby's ear to listen to us, but has also awakened him to correction. We wholeheartedly believe our baby hears when you call him by his name from the womb; you have had him in your memory and engraved yourself in his memory from his mother's bowels.

LORD, if our baby is a boy, make his production of spermatozoa and testosterone like a fountain, a well of living waters and streams from Lebanon. Father, we pray for you to take care of the formation of his eyelids. May they effectively perform the function of protecting his eyes and moisturizing them. Protect his nails, so they will be free from fungus and not easily broken, but on the contrary, need to be trimmed.

Now that his brain has entered a stage of rapid growth, we ask you to do him justice, assuring that each cell moves to the corresponding place in his brain, making the necessary connections for his development. We pray that each of the five senses will be perfectly developed to enable learning.

We trust you to engrave in his brain the Word we have been praying over him. May the Word anchor him to instruction, to acquire wisdom, gain intelligence and never forget or depart from the words of your mouth. We prophesy he will never let go of your Word; he will keep it because it will be health for his body. In the name of Jesus, we pray. Amen!

Prayer Guide for the Soul of Our Baby (emotions – mind – will)

LORD, you are Our Righteousness. We thank you for your goodness and ask that goodness, fruit of the Holy Spirit flourish in our baby's heart. From the womb, may our baby's face contemplate your glory, as if in a mirror and be transformed into the very image of your glory.

May he understand the purpose of his teaching is love, born from a pure heart, from a good conscience and from a sincere faith. We ask that the Word we are praying over our baby permeate his soul to create a total dependence on you, to help him discern the difference between the just and the wicked, the one who serves God and the one who doesn't. Let him be a doer of the Word and not just a hearer. Allow his heart to be full of goodness and understand that the fruit of the light consist of all goodness, justice and truth. May his desire be to imitate you.

Give him a kind and generous heart to perform deeds of goodness, without partiality, just like Dorcas. Help him recognize that pure and undefiled religion before you is to visit orphans and widows in their distress and to keep oneself untainted by the world. We prophesy he will be known as a servant of Christ and administrator of the mysteries of God. In the name of Jesus, we pray. Amen!

Prayer Guide for the Spirit of Our Baby

Our most beloved baby, in the name of Jesus Christ, we now speak to your spirit. Listen carefully to what the Word of God says: "So says Jehovah: If you can invalidate my covenant with the day and my covenant with the night, that there will not be day and night at their appointed time, then also my covenant with my servant David may be broken, that he will not have a son to reign on his throne and my covenant with the Levites and priests, my ministers."

Baby, God loves you; listen to what he tells you: "Because he is our God; we are the people of his meadow, and the sheep of his hand." Baby, God loves you and because he loves you so much, he thought of all your needs and made provision for you to live a victorious life in him, in the midst of a fallen world where people love darkness. This is why we have begun to teach you and bless you from your mother's womb.

We bless you with the conviction and tenacity of knowing that although you walk in the flesh, you do not wrestle according to the flesh. In the name of Jesus, we bless you with a spirit strengthened in the Word of God, capable of casting aside the deeds of darkness and dressed with the weapons of light. We bless you with the wisdom of knowing that the weapons of our warfare are not of the flesh but powerful in God for the destruction of fortresses. We bless you with a path marked by the Word of God. In the name of Jesus, we pray. Amen!

Week 23: I am alive and I describe my development.
I measure approximately 11.38 inches (28.9 cm)
long and weigh about 1.1 lbs (501 g).

Thank you, Father, because you continue to talk to my heart like a gentle breeze, as the proportions of my body become similar to those of a newborn child. Although fat has accumulated in my body, my skin still hangs loosely, giving me a wrinkled appearance. Wrinkles, what a horror! Glory to God they'll soon disappear!

The bones of the middle ear have hardened and I can hear well. Daddy, did you know that your masculine, low pitched voice, is special and penetrates the abdomen and the uterus much better than Mommy's high pitched feminine voice? My eyes are formed, but the iris still has no pigmentation. I imagine you continue to ask yourselves what color eyes I have and who I will look like. You will have to wait several weeks before you know.

My pancreas, a vital organ in the production of hormones, is developing continually and has begun to produce insulin, an important substance to process sugar.

If I were to be born this 23rd week, I would have a 15 percent probability of survival; therefore, although I have a great desire to see you, I'll stay in my little house for several more weeks.

I forgot to tell you something, Mommy. I have my own daily exercise routine. This routine includes regularly moving the muscles of my arms, my legs, my fingers and toes. So, if you feel some vigorous movements, which in no way feel like a gentle breeze, all I can say is that I am sorry; but, you know I must exercise to stay in shape.

Prayer Guide for the Physical Development of Our Baby

Father, how beautiful is your gentle voice which quiets us and gives us the confidence of knowing that all the days of our baby are written in your book of life. We know our baby has been created by you and the day of his birth is being closely guarded by you.

Dear God, we know your gentle whisper has opened our baby's ear and is nourishing the growth of his joints and ligaments. We declare, like Job, as his muscles and internal organs are being formed, his strength is in his back and his vigor in the muscles of his belly. Therefore, each internal organ functions perfectly.

We ask you to care for the iris of his eyes; we thank you for the color you have chosen for its pigmentation. Father, we pray you would cover the formation of our baby's pancreas with your blood. May his pancreas be healthy, capable of fulfilling its hormonal function and of producing insulin for as long as his body has the breath of life. In the name of Jesus, we pray. Amen!

Prayer Guide for the Soul of Our Baby (emotions – mind – will)

Lord, we declare your presence is manifested in our baby like the tender whisper of a gentle breeze that calms the soul, delights the heart and provokes a response from men. Let his response be like the centurion, who moved by love and compassion, approached Jesus imploring him to heal his servant who was bedridden, paralyzed and suffering. Father, may the Word we are praying for our baby be planted and treasured in his heart by the power of the Holy Spirit. We pray that goodness, fruit of the Holy Spirit, mold his character and strongly manifest itself in his life. May his life be characterized by acts of goodness toward his fellow man, as the centurion with his servant.

LORD, the longing of our hearts is that you whisper your wisdom into his ear and you incline his heart to understanding; for your Word establishes that you give wisdom and from your mouth comes knowledge and intelligence. We prophesy he will cry out to intelligence, lift his voice to understanding, seek it as silver and search for it as for hidden treasure; he will then understand the fear of the LORD and discover the knowledge of God. Give him a heart according to yours, for we know you are a merciful and gracious

God, slow to anger, abundant in mercy, loving kindness and truth. In the name of Jesus, we pray. Amen!

Prayer Guide for the Spirit of Our Baby

Baby, we want you to listen carefully with your spirit to what God says about you. In the name of Jesus Christ we raise our voices directly to your spirit to read the Word of God to you: "Therefore, take up the full armor of God, so that you will be able to resist in the evil day, and having finished everything, stand firm." Baby, as we have already told you, there will be bad days in your life; therefore, it will be necessary for you to be clothed with the full armor of God to resist, and having done so, stand firm.

Dear baby, during the following weeks we will be teaching you about the powerful spiritual clothing, called God's armor, which he has prepared for you. This clothing will grow with you like the clothes of God's people when they left Egypt, which never grew old or deteriorated. It radiates the grace and beauty of our God, and at the same time will protect you from the inside out. It not only adds beauty to your appearance but also reflects the beauty of your Creator. This clothing must be worn at all times for it to become part of your being. It is clothing the enemy of your soul will see upon you, for it reflects the light of Jesus. Once you take possession of it and make it part of your being, it will give you a new confidence and conviction that he who fights in your favor is more powerful than he who is against you.

Baby, we bless you with spiritual discernment for your sense of hearing, smell, touch, taste and vision, so they will be alert to discern the deceptions of the enemy. We bless you with being guided by the Holy Spirit, to know that you should always be dressed with your spiritual clothing. We bless you with the understanding that this clothing, which God calls his armor, will protect you during the bad days. This armor of God will protect you during the spiritual, emotional and physical attacks of the forces of evil. We bless you with the knowledge of knowing when to assume a spiritual defensive position and when to assume an offensive position. We bless you with the peace, joy, love, hope and victory that are yours in Christ Jesus. Amen!

Week 24:I am alive and I describe my development. I measure approximately 11.8 inches (30 cm) long and weigh about 1.3 lbs (600 g).

The beauty of the Ancient of Days is upon me; he is making me beautiful as I continue to gain weight. Relax, you won't have to put me on a diet, its only six ounces distributed in muscle, bone mass and organs. This increase in weight beautifies me and makes my appearance look more like a newborn.

My taste buds continue to form. Mommy, did you know that when you eat or drink something strange or bitter, I will perceive it?

Small creases have formed in the palms of my hands. My muscular coordination has improved while I suck my thumb. During the next seven days, my sweat glands will be forming in my skin; don't worry! This doesn't mean you must go out to buy deodorant for me; for I am still like the fragrance of Christ to God among those who are saved, as well as among those who perish.

My lungs are developing pulmonary alveoli, which are like the respiratory branches of a tree. They are also producing the cells that generate surfactant. The surfactant is a substance that helps the pulmonary alveoli fill up with air easily, so they won't stick together when we exhale, allowing us to breathe correctly.

Since my middle ear, which controls the balance of the body, is completely developed, I may know when I am facing up or facing down, as I float and do my acrobatics inside Mommy's tummy. If I were to be born this week, I would have higher probabilities of surviving; but, I like my little house. I am not thinking about leaving it just yet.

Prayer Guide for the Physical Growth of Our Baby

The beauty of the Ancient of Days is unequal and man was made in the image of God; therefore, whether our baby is a boy or a girl, we know it will be beautiful. We raise our voices and bless the physical development of our baby, declaring his hands are like gold bars set in topaz, his belly carved ivory inlaid with sapphires, his legs columns of alabaster set on pedestals of pure gold, his appearance like Lebanon, and graceful like the cedars, his palate sweet and he is wholly desirable. Our baby will be beautiful! His eyes are as doves.

Oh Ancient of Days, we have surrendered our baby to you. From the womb, you are his God. Allow his palate to taste with zest, like your children tasted the manna in the desert and found it was sweet, like flakes with honey and called it "manna." We declare that his lungs are strong and free from any pulmonary disease. In the name of Jesus, we pray. Amen!

Prayer Guide for the Soul of Our Baby (emotions – mind – will)

You are the Ancient of Days, he who doesn't change and whose years will not come to an end. To you and to you alone we entrust the life of our baby. May God the Father and Jesus Christ our LORD direct his steps onto his old age, and sustain him even in his advanced years. May he listen to your voice, you be his God and he walk in all the paths you lead him so it will be well with him.

We prophesy that his soul will cling to you; your right hand will sustain him and let him know the path of life. In your presence he will know abundance of joy and delights forever. Like a mantle you will roll him up in your presence so his character is free of greed. He will share with others and reflect goodness, fruit of the Holy Spirit.

Allow our baby's heart to be like the heart of Joseph of Arimathea, who used his influence to go before Pilate and requested the body of Jesus. Then, taking the body of Jesus, he wrapped it up in a clean linen cloth and laid it in a new tomb that belonged to him. In like manner, may our baby always be attentive to the needs of others, willing to help the weak, remembering the words of Jesus who said: "It is more blessed to give than to receive." In the name of Jesus, we pray. Amen!

Prayer Guide for the Spirit of Our Baby

Baby, just as we have continued praying for your physical development and your soul, we continue praying for the most important part of your whole being, your spirit. During this week, we are going to teach you about another piece of the armor of God. Therefore, baby, listen with your spirit to what God is telling you: "Therefore, stand firm, having girded your loins with the truth." Baby, there is so much to tell you about this piece; but, for the moment, we'll just teach you the basic fundamentals. The first thing you should know is that to gird your loins with truth means to believe that the LORD is the only true God. For God so loved the world that he gave Jesus, his only begotten son, so whoever believes in him shall not perish but have eternal life. Baby, God already showed his love for us and desires for you to love him with all your being. Spirit of our baby, listen to this great truth: "Jesus said: I am the way and the truth and the life, no one comes to the Father but through me." Baby, in the name of Jesus, we bless your spirit with spiritual discernment for you to be able to understand the scriptures when it says: "In that day you will know that I am in my Father, and you in me, and I in you. He who has my commandments, and keeps them, is the one who loves me; and he who loves me will be loved by my Father, and I will love him and will disclose myself to him."

We bless you with the understanding that Christ is in the Father and that as soon as you surrender your life to Jesus, your life will be hidden in him and he will be with you through the Holy Spirit. We bless you with a profound revelation of the truth of the Word, of how much God loves you, and the necessity to obey his commandments. We bless you with the truth that Jesus reigns over all the powers in the air. We bless you with the spiritual understanding that God himself is your spiritual armor. In the name of Jesus Christ. Amen!

Week 25: I am alive and I describe my development. I measure approximately 13.6 inches (34.6 cm) long and weigh about 1.46 lbs (660 g).

This week the Rock of Israel is forming the structure of my spinal column, its joints, ligaments and discs. These are the ones that will protect my spinal cord, which serve as transmitters of information to all of my body. The blood vessels in my body are developing. My nasal cavities begin to open and it is believed that I can already show a preference to certain smells. The nerves around my mouth and my lips are now more sensitive. My swallowing reflexes are developing. My skills have improved. Now I not only do acrobatics, but I'm starting to make a fist and can grab objects placed in the palm of my hand. I long to show you how strongly I can grab your fingers if you put them in the palm of my hand! I will continue to practice until that great day comes!

Prayer Guide for the Physical Growth of Our Baby

There are songs in our hearts, like in the nights when feasts are celebrated. There is joy of heart, like when one marches to the sound of a flute, as we come closer to our LORD, to the Rock of Israel. Our trust is in you, the Rock of Our Salvation. Dear LORD, we believe you have formed the spinal column of our baby and have given the order for bone with bone, disc with disc, and ligament with ligament to be joined together. Just as the breastplate of the Levites was held together by rings with a blue cord to the belt of the ephod, so it would remain in its place, in this same manner protect the spinal cord of our baby so that it may flourish like a palm and grow strong like a cedar in Lebanon.

Father, your Word establishes that the life of the flesh is in the blood; therefore, we ask you to protect each of our baby's blood vessels. Let them efficiently carry out their function of conducting the blood propelled by the action of the heart. We declare you have formed his nostrils, your breath is in his nose and you will be a pleasing fragrance to him. Thank you for forming each nerve around his mouth and lips, for making sure he will have no trouble in swallowing, for giving him strong muscles like the buffalo and for anointing him with fresh oil. In the name of Jesus, we pray. Amen!

Prayer Guide for the Soul of Our Baby (emotions – mind – will)

We sing with joy to the LORD; we acclaim with jubilation to the Rock of Our Salvation. We come before his presence with thanksgiving. For you are our God; and we are the people of your pasture and the lambs of your hand. We declare our baby hears your voice from his mother's womb. He will not harden his heart but with a sincere heart he will bless you at all times; and your praise shall continually be in his mouth.

In you, oh LORD, his soul will glory; the humble will hear him and will rejoice. He will invite others to magnify you and exalt your name. He will declare your loving goodness in the morning and your faithfulness at night. He will not be like a senseless man who has no knowledge or the fool who doesn't understand. Rather, he will be like Rahab, who did not perish together with the disobedient. Realizing that the spies were God's ambassadors, she was good to them, even risking her own life for them. She not only thought of her own well-being, but showed her loving goodness by interceding for her family. Rock of Israel, just as your blessing was upon Rahab and she was included in the maternal line of Christ's predecessors, may our baby be planted in your house. May he flourish in your courts as the palm flourishes and the cedar grows in Lebanon, so even in his old age he bears fruit, is vigorous and very green. In the name of Jesus, we pray. Amen!

Prayer Guide for the Spirit of Our Baby

Baby, we direct our voices to your spirit in the name of Jesus Christ. During this week, we will teach you about another piece of God's clothing of truth at your disposition. Listen to this truth with your spirit; it comes directly from the Word of God: "Know, therefore, today, and reflect in your heart, that Jehovah is God in heaven above and on the earth below, and there is no other." Baby, as we have already told you, our God is one and we want you to reflect on this truth. He is God up in heaven and down on earth, aside from him there is no other God!

Another important thing you should know is that we have an adversary. Baby, listen with your spirit to how God describes him: "He has been a murderer from the beginning, and has not stayed in the truth, because there is no truth in him. Whenever he speaks a lie, he speaks from his own nature, for he is a liar and the father of lies." Baby, the father of lies is our adversary; he is a thief and his mission is to rob, to kill and destroy. The father of lies will want to snatch the truth from your life. This is why God teaches us that truth has to be fastened to our waist.

Baby, we bless you with receiving the truth and treasuring the commandments of God. May your ear be attentive to wisdom and your heart inclined to understanding. If you cry for discernment and lift your voice to understanding, if you seek it as silver and search for it as for hidden treasures, then you will discern the fear of the LORD and discover the knowledge of God. For the LORD gives wisdom; from his mouth comes knowledge and understanding. In the name of Jesus, Christ we pray. Amen!

Week 26:I am alive and I describe my development. I measure approximately 14 inches (35.6 cm) long and weigh about 1.7 lbs (760 g).

Strong Tower is the name of my LORD. He is the one that makes my spinal cord stronger; it already has 150 joints, 33 discs and some 1,000 ligaments. My lungs continue to develop and begin to secrete surfactant, which will cover the alveolus in my lungs.

My eyes will start to open and blink during this week. The retina of my eyes begins to form. My eyelashes start to grow and more hair grows on my head. Perhaps, when I am born, I will need a haircut. Brain activity for hearing and vision begins to be detected. A scan of my brain would show my response to touch. If you shine a bright light on Mommy's tummy, I will turn my head toward it because, according to researchers, my optic nerve perceives it.

Prayer Guide for the Physical Development of Our Baby

Strong Tower is the name of our LORD; to him the righteous runs and is safe. This is why we know our baby is safe. His spinal cord and neck are like an ivory tower. We believe you place eyelashes as veils to protect his eyes and make them beautiful; from the womb, you uncover his eyes so he can see you, the light of the world.

We thank you for taking care of the abundant activity going on inside our baby's brain for his hearing and vision. Allow our baby to be healthy, sensitive to touch, with sharp vision and hearing; but above all, to be sensitive to your voice and your presence. Give him lungs as strong as yours, that with one breath you cleanse the heavens.

Beloved God, we present you with the initial formation of the retina of the eyes of our baby, the tissue sensitive to light which will trigger a series of chemical and electrical phenomena that become nerve impulses sent to the brain by the optic nerve, resulting in the formation of the image our baby will perceive. As we pray for our baby, we ask you, the light of the world to enlighten his eyes and personally form the retina. In the name of Jesus, we pray. Amen!

Prayer Guide for the Soul of Our Baby
(emotions – mind – will)

Strong Tower is the name of our LORD; to him the righteous runs and is safe. We will meditate in the glorious splendor of your majesty and your wonderful deeds. We will speak about the power of your marvelous deeds and will tell about your greatness.

Compassionate and merciful are you, oh LORD, slow to anger and great in mercy. You are good with all and your compassion is over all your deeds. Since our baby is the work of your hands, and you are a loving and kind God, we believe that from the womb, the seed of goodness, fruit of the Spirit, will be planted in his heart.

We prophesy that as he listens to your voice, goodness will emanate from his heart and produce good deeds toward others. He will listen to your voice and begin to thank you and bless you; unto his old age he will proclaim with enthusiasm, the memory of your great goodness and sing with joy of your righteousness.

We pray his ways are affirmed to keep your statutes; for, we know that in considering all of your commandments he will not be ashamed, and with an upright heart he will thank you, having learned your righteous trials. May he search for you with all his heart and never part from your commandments, but treasure your Word and sin not against you. In the name of Jesus, we pray. Amen!

Prayer Guide for the Spirit of Our Baby

Spirit of our baby, we speak to you in the name of Jesus Christ. Listen carefully to each word we will be speaking to you. Our heart's desire is to teach you, from your mother's womb, about the spiritual clothing God has provided for you. Baby, in the name of Jesus, listen with your spirit to what the Word of God says: "Stand firm, therefore, having girded your loins with truth, having put on the breastplate of righteousness." Baby, to be dressed with the breastplate of righteousness means that freely and by his grace, once you give your heart to Jesus, you receive salvation through the redemption in Christ Jesus. Baby, God already made provision for your salvation, but to enjoy so great a gift as salvation, you first need to surrender your heart to Jesus and once you have done this, clothe yourself with God's righteousness.

Baby, God is good and he knows how deceitful the heart is, and as the water reflects the face, so the heart of man reflects man. In light of this reality, God warns us saying: "Watch over your heart with all diligence, for from it flow the springs of life."

Baby, we believe your spirit receives each word we have prayed over you. You will be like Josiah, who at the age of eight began to reign and did right in the sight of the LORD. He walked in the ways of his father David; he did not turn to the right or to the left. We believe that at an early age, you will give your heart to God and your eyes will delight in his ways.

May God establish you, anoint you, seal you, and give his spirit to your heart, as a pledge of your salvation. We pray God's laws will be in your heart and your steps will not falter. May your delight be to do the will of God and his law to be in your heart. Father, we ask you to create a clean heart and a steadfast spirit within our baby. Teach him, Oh LORD, your way, for him to walk in your truth unite his heart to fear your name. Give him understanding to observe your law and obey it with all his heart. May he, forever, take your testimonies as an inheritance, so he will be a joy to your heart; incline his heart to comply with your statutes forever and to the end. In the name of Jesus, Christ. Amen!

Seventh Month

Weeks 27-30

Summary of the Pregnancy Process

Week 27: Hearing continues to be refined. The retina is formed.

Week 28: Eyebrows and eyelashes are clearly visible. The hair is growing. The eyes are completely formed. Baby continues to gain weight, primarily in bone and muscular density. The lungs are capable of breathing. The baby can recognize sounds. The baby's blood changes and is capable of carrying its own oxygen.

Week 29: The brain now controls the breathing and the temperature of the body.

Week 30: The red blood cells carry oxygen and remove waste (carbon monoxide and other gases).

The Prayer Focus Will Be:

Week	Name of God	Bible Character	Prayer Focus The Soul	Prayer Focus The Spirit
27.	God of Seeing	Abraham	Fruit of Faithfulness	Footwear of the Gospel of Peace
28.	Father	Joshua	Fruit of Faithfulness	The Shield of Faith
29.	Redeemer	Mary, the Mother of Jesus	Fruit of Faithfulness	The Helmet of Salvation
30.	I AM WHO I AM	Jehosheba	Fruit of Faithfulness	Sword of the Spirit

The Festivals of Israel and Pregnancy

The Festivals of Israel	Pregnancy
Feast of Trumpets *Lev 23:24:* "Speak unto the children of Israel, saying, 'In the seventh month, in the first day of the month, shall ye have a Sabbath, a memorial of blowing of trumpets, a holy convocation."	**Hearing Recognition** The first day of the seventh month, the baby's hearing is completely developed. He can distinguish sound for what it really is, for example, the sound of a trumpet.
Feast of Atonement *Lev 23:27:* "Also on the tenth day of this seventh month there shall be a day of atonement: it shall be a holy convocation unto you; and ye shall afflict your souls, and offer an offering made by fire unto the Lord."	**The Baby's Blood Changes** During the 2nd week of the seventh month, on the 10th day to be exact, the baby's blood begins to produce hemoglobin. He will no longer depend on his mother's oxygen, for he can now produce his own oxygen.
Feast of Tabernacles *Lev 23:34:* "Speak unto the children of Israel, saying, The fifteenth day of this seventh month shall be the feast of tabernacles for seven days unto the Lord."	**The Lungs are Sufficiently Developed to Function** On the 15th day of the seventh month the lungs are sufficiently developed to begin functioning. **Note:** The Tabernacle is the house of the spirit and the spirit is represented by air.

Week 27: I am alive and I describe my development. I measure approximately 14.4 inches (36.6 cm) long and weigh about 1.9 lbs (875 g).

Hallelujah! You are the God who sees; and by your grace I have begun to see. My eyelids are more open and I can distinguish light from darkness. The retina of my eyes is developed.

My appearance is similar to what I'll look like at birth, except that I'm thinner and smaller. My lungs, liver and immune system still need to mature. If I were to be born this week, my possibilities of surviving would be very good; but as you know, I don't plan to leave my little house yet. I like the little house my Creator made for me.

As my hearing continues to develop, I begin to recognize Mommy's and Daddy's voices. The sounds are muffled because my ears are still covered with vernix, a waxy substance that protects my skin and prevents it from becoming chapped by the amniotic fluid. My Creator thought of everything; I even have my own moisturizer.

My brain continues to grow rapidly. I need for you to talk to me, play music and repeatedly read the same books to me. My hearing is becoming more refined; next week the whole network of nerves for my ears will be complete. My lungs continue to develop and are preparing to function outside of my little house; meanwhile, I practice breathing small portions of liquid from my personal pool.

Prayer Guide for the Physical Development of Our Baby

We recognize you are the God that sees. Thank you for taking care of our baby's eyesight and for the formation of the retina, responsible for the images our baby will perceive. We ask you to bestow upon his eyes the same blessing you gave to your servant Moses, who was 120 years old when he died, and his vision had not diminished nor his vigor reduced.

Thank you for beautifying our baby. We trust if it's a girl, she'll be as beautiful as Sarah, Abraham's wife, and if it's a boy he will be good looking, like Absalom. Beloved God, your Word says you created man from the dust of the earth; you blew the breath of life into his nostrils and he became a living being. We believe it was you who also blew the breath of life into our baby; and we are thankful.

Dear LORD, cover with your shadow, his lungs, kidneys and other organs, still in development. Allow his lungs to be strong and perfectly perform their job of supplying oxygen to the blood. Likewise, allow his liver to produce and eliminate bile, metabolize carbohydrates and fat, handle the formation or synthesizing of proteins, the formation or synthesizing of the coagulation factors and the detoxification of his blood. As you cared for your people when you brought them out of Egypt, setting aside all type of disease, allow our baby's immune system to become an impenetrable wall, keeping out all disease. Give it the ability to identify and attack pathogenic organisms.

Thank you for caring for his hearing. We pray that just as Samuel heard your voice when you called, even though your Word was scarce in those days, our baby will hear and recognize your voice from his mother's womb. May his heart rejoice when your lips speak to him. We thank you for covering and protecting his skin with his own moisturizer. We pray you will protect the multiple neurological connections being formed in his brain. Give him of your intelligence; for we know the LORD gives wisdom and out of his mouth comes knowledge and intelligence. In the name of Jesus, we pray. Amen!

Prayer Guide for the Soul of Our Baby (emotions – mind – will)

Blessed are you, the God that sees and to whom nothing is hidden. Our eyes look to you oh GOD, and in you we are sheltered. Our hearts overflow with joy because we know your eyes have been over our baby since the very day of his conception. For this reason, we join our voices to the voices in heaven proclaiming: "You are worthy, our LORD and God, of receiving the glory, and the honor and the power because you created all things, and by your will they exist and were created."

Good LORD, we ask for faithfulness, fruit of the Holy Spirit, to overflow in the life of our baby. Raise him up as a faithful priest to you, who will do according to your heart's desire. Edify a lasting house for him, and may he always walk before you. Let his heart be like Abraham's, whom you, the LORD God, chose because you found his heart to be faithful before you. You made a covenant with him to give him the land of the Canaanites, Hittites, Amorites, Perizzites, Jebusites and the Girgashites, to give it to his descendants. You kept your word, because you are just.

We pray your Word will flourish in him so when he opens his mouth he will make known with boldness the mystery of the gospel. We proclaim that regardless of the circumstances surrounding him, he will never be ashamed of the gospel. He will have the conviction that the message of the cross is nonsense for the lost but is the power of God for salvation to everyone who believes. In the name of Jesus, we pray. Amen!

Prayer Guide for the Spirit of Our Baby

Baby, we want you to listen carefully with your spirit to what God says about you. Therefore, in the name of Jesus, we speak directly to your spirit: "Blessed be the God and Father of our Lord Jesus Christ, who has blessed us with every spiritual blessing in the heavenly places in Christ, just as He chose us in Him before the foundation of the world, that we would be holy and blameless before Him. In love He predestined us to adoption as sons through Jesus Christ to Himself, according to the kind intention of His will."

Baby, we, your parents bless you with the certainty that you are a beloved child of God; he knows you and created you to give glory to his name. We bless you with the ability to hear his voice and know the design of God for your life. We bless you with a teachable spirit, which recognizes that its identity is in Jesus Christ and only in Christ will you be able to fulfill your destiny and find fullness of life.

We declare, from your mother's womb, your feet are shod with the preparation to announce the gospel of peace. To walk in the peace of God is an act of the will. The peace of God is a great treasure, which the world does not recognize. We pray the circumstances of the world will not confuse your heart or fear overcome you. We pray you will know the Prince of Peace and your feet will always be shod with this part of the armor of God. We bless you with peace and an evangelistic spirit that emanates from you, and leads others to desire to know more about the Prince of Peace. We bless you with a walk full of the presence of God, where your daily conversations will give him glory. We bless you with the feet of one who brings good news of great joy, with simplicity, so people will understand, believe, repent and surrender their lives to Christ. In the name of Jesus Christ we pray. Amen!

Week 28: I am alive and I describe my development. I measure approximately 14.8 inches (37.6 cm) long and weigh about 2.2 lbs (1,005 g).

My God determined that he would be a father to me and that I would be his son. He built a little house inside of my Mommy's womb. He continues to miraculously interweave my body.

The folds and grooves of my brain continue their growth and expansion. My God continues to deposit his intelligence in me. You'd be surprised of all of the things I'm capable of doing at this tender age. My eyes are fully formed; my eyebrows and eyelashes are clearly visible. I can bat my eyelashes and perhaps you'll see them on your next visit to the doctor. My hair is growing. I'm sure you're anxious to discover who I look like, and the color of my eyes and hair. Be patient just a little bit longer. It is best that I stay a little longer in my little transitory house, the one the Father made for me. In the meantime, I continue to gain weight, mostly in bone and muscle density.

As I do my daily routine of exercise, inside my little house, you'll notice my muscle tone continues to improve; it may feel like I am preparing for the Olympics. My lungs are capable of breathing; but, I'm still not ready to breathe on my own outside of my little house. I can recognize your voices and I like listening to you. I like it when you pray, read and sing to me. Listening to your voices helps me to relax.

Prayer Guide for the Physical Development of Our Baby

Loving Father, our hearts rejoice and worship the greatness of your name and the love you have for your children. You are wonderful! Our hearts know it very well. The miracle of conception and development of our baby is your doing, a God that has identified himself as father of orphans and does not abandon his children.

Our limited knowledge does not comprehend the way of the spirit or how the bones grow in the womb of a pregnant woman.

What we do know is that the formation and development of our baby has not been out of your sight. It has been you, as a loving father, who majestically interwove him inside his mother's womb. For this we praise you. Amazing and wonderful are your deeds and our souls know it quite well. We ask you to weave your wisdom and intelligence into the most intimate part of each fold and groove of his brain and also beautify his physical features. Give him eyes, like those of a dove. We declare, from the womb his eyes will look to you. Give him beautiful and abundant hair like Absalom's and a heart like David's. His muscles will be strengthened; for you are his strength and his shield; therefore, his heart will rejoice.

We prophesy that your voice is known to him; and his lungs are strengthened because you looked upon them. Each breath our baby takes is a song of gratitude for his loving Father who has brought him to the banquet hall and your standard over him is love. In the name of Jesus, we pray. Amen!

Prayer Guide for the Soul of Our Baby (emotions – mind – will)

Oh LORD, you are our father and we thank you for loving us the way you do and for modeling the love of a father. We depend on your faithfulness for knowledge to raise our child, and trust you have revealed yourself to him as his loving father. We ask you to sustain him and secure him, so he may continually pay attention to your decrees. Be his hiding place and shield. Keep evildoers away from him and help him to keep your commandments.

Father, we ask you to prepare him to fulfill your purpose in his life. Allow him to be bold and strong. As Joshua, may he know how to serve and surrender faithfully to the mentors you place in his life. Sustain him according to your promise so that he lives and will never be ashamed of you, his hope.

May the seed of faithfulness, fruit of the Holy Spirit, be firmly rooted in him and his eyes stay focused on the things above and not on the things of this earth. Open his mind to comprehend the scriptures, to long for your salvation and for your law to be his delight.

We decree that at an early age he will surrender his life to you, die to the things of the world, and his life will be hidden with Christ in God. Give him the conviction that when Christ, who is our life, is revealed then he will also be revealed with him in glory. Therefore, he will consider the members of his earthly body as dead to fornication, impurity, passion, evil desire and greed, which is idolatry.

We know your hand will always be ready to help him, for he has chosen your precepts. Oh Father, as one of your sons, allow his tongue to sing your Word because all your commandments are righteous; may his soul live to praise you and your ordinances to guide him. In the name of Jesus, we pray. Amen!

Prayer Guide for the Spirit of Our Baby

Our very beloved baby, in the name of Jesus Christ, we now speak to your spirit. Listen carefully, for we are going to speak to you about another piece of the armor, which God has prepared for you. It is called the shield of faith. Listen with your spirit to what God's Word says about this piece of the armor: "Above all, take up the shield of faith with which you will be able to extinguish all the flaming arrows of the evil one."

Baby, a shield is a defensive weapon used to cover and protect oneself from an attack. Faith is to believe with all certainty that what you are waiting for will come to pass. Also, it is an offensive weapon with which one can attack the enemy and defeat him. Therefore, with the shield of faith you will able to extinguish any doubt concerning the promises God has made to you.

Baby, each prayer we have said has been an act of faith. We are convinced that although we can't see your spirit, it is being quickened by the power of the Word we are praying over you. The Word tells us that faith comes by hearing, and hearing comes by the Word of God, and the righteousness of God is revealed by faith and for faith.

By faith we believe we are establishing a shield of protection around you. By faith, not by sight, we believe God is a shield to all who take refuge in him. He is a shield around you, your glory, and the one who raises your head.

Baby, the Word of God declares to those who adore and trust him, that he is their help and their shield. He will bless those who fear him, young and old. Baby, listen carefully with your spirit to what the Word of God tells you about faith: "But without faith it is impossible to please God, because it is necessary that he who comes near God believes that he is, and that he is the rewarder of those who seek him." We bless you with the capacity to believe as Abraham, who believed in hope against hope. We bless you with an unshakable faith in the Word of God, with the complete conviction that what God has promised he is powerful to fulfill; therefore, your faith will be credited to you as righteousness. In the name of Jesus Christ we pray. Amen!

Week 29: I am alive and I describe my development. I measure approximately 15.2 inches (38.6 cm) long and weigh about 2.54 lbs (1,153 g).

My Redeemer lives and takes care of me. I am beautiful and I no longer look like an alien. My head is now proportional to the rest of my body and my appearance is that of a newborn baby.

I continue to gain weight as I prepare to leave my little transitional home to be received in the arms of the family My Redeemer chose for me. I can already imagine how our first encounter will be. I will be like an antidote; Mommy will forget all her labor pains. Mommy and Daddy will examine me from top to bottom and cry with joy as they thank my Creator. Isn't that exciting? It will definitely be love at first sight.

My brain already controls my respiration and body temperature. My eyes move; soon I'll be able to follow a blinking light. I already show a preference to certain scents and flavors. My sensitivity to changes in light, sound, taste and scent has also increased. I continue to keep an exercise schedule by moving from side to side and doing acrobatics. I need to stay in shape. Who knows if someday I'll be dancing for My Redeemer? My head continues to be in an upright position.

Prayer Guide for the Physical Development of Our Baby

Oh, our Redeemer, your hands formed our baby. As we pray for our child, allow him to understand and learn your commandments. Thank you for making him a living soul, for his formation, for each detail you have crafted in his physical body and for his new born appearance.

We ask that, as Elisha prayed for the eyes of his servant to be opened to the spiritual world to see how you, our Redeemer, who fights in our favor, the physical eyes and ears of our baby will receive the order to be opened to see and hear.

Beloved Redeemer, our baby is a manifestation of the work done by you. Since you are the light of the world and whoever follows you will not walk in darkness, he will have the light of life. We ask that as his sensitivity to light increases, your light would shine upon him. May he open his mouth and sigh because he desires your commandments. While his physical senses are being carefully developed, may his spiritual senses also develop, causing his hearing to examine every word. As the palate tastes food, cause the words of his Redeemer to be sweeter than honey to his palate.

Being that your children are the fragrance of Christ to God, permit our baby to be a manifestation of the fragrance of your knowledge wherever he goes. Blessed is the man whose strength is in you, in whose heart are your ways; we declare that the strength of our baby to perform each movement comes from his Redeemer. In the name of Jesus, we pray. Amen!

Prayer Guide for the Soul of Our Baby (emotions – mind – will)

We know our Redeemer lives and this is the covenant he has established: "He will put his laws in our minds and write them in our hearts." Redeemer, we claim these promises for our baby. We ask for the seed of faithfulness, fruit of the Holy Spirit, to be planted in his heart. Just as Mary, Jesus' mother, received your words, treasured them, and remained faithful to you, may our baby also remain faithful to you. We prophesy that regardless of the circumstances he may encounter, just as Mary, our baby will be of those of firm purpose. He will persist in the things he has learned, convinced of whom he has learned them from. From his mother's womb he will know the Holy Scriptures, which will lead him to salvation through faith in Jesus Christ, and to be equipped for every good deed.

Beloved God, we ask you to give him the speech of a disciple, so he may know how to sustain the weary one with a precise word.

Awaken his ear each morning to listen to the sayings of your mouth. We declare the words from his mouth and the meditations of his heart will be pleasing to God. Our baby will be the fragrant aroma of Christ among those who are saved and among those who are perishing. Wisdom will enter his heart and knowledge will be pleasing to his soul.

We prophesy our baby is part of the generation of those who seek your face. Your precepts will gladden his heart and your commandments illuminate his eyes. Your laws are engraved in his mind and written in his heart, for your perfect law restores his soul and makes him wise. In the name of Jesus, we pray. Amen!

Prayer Guide for the Spirit of Our Baby

Spirit of our baby, we speak to you in the name of Jesus Christ. Listen carefully to each word we speak to you. We want to feed you with the Word of God and continue teaching you about another part of the powerful armor God makes available to you. Baby, listen with your spirit to the Word of God: "And take the helmet of salvation." A helmet is used to protect the head. Baby, in your walk through life, Satan, your enemy, will try to attack your thoughts and make you doubt the love of God and the salvation plan he has provided for those who accept Jesus as their savior.

Our prayer is that at a very early age you will surrender your heart to God so you will be clothed with the new man, in the likeness of God, created in righteousness and the holiness of the truth. Your mind will not be led away from the purity and simplicity of the devotion to Christ.

We pray you will have the conviction of salvation and spiritual knowledge of the greatness of the salvation Christ has earned for those who accept him as their savior. We declare the certainty of salvation will preserve you in the day of conflict and extinguish the flaming arrows of the enemy.

Baby, we prophesy you will know the greatness of your salvation in Christ. Your hope will not be on the things you see but in the Word of God, which establishes that through the Holy Spirit God comes and makes a dwelling place in you and has affirmed that he will never leave you. In the name of Jesus, we pray. Amen!

Week 30: I am alive and I describe my development. I measure approximately 15.7 inches (39.9 cm) long and weigh about 2.9 lbs (1,319 g).

The great I AM WHO I AM has sent me to you. Look at how much I've grown inside of my little house; I weight nearly 3 pounds. It's a wonder how I manage to position myself in this small space which is getting smaller every day. It's all those acrobatics I continue to practice. I tell you, I can qualify to compete in the next Olympics!

I am also a beauty. My toenails are entering the final stage of growth. My hair continues to grow. My bone marrow is now responsible for the production of my red blood cells. Don't stop praying for it, since these cells carry oxygen and remove waste (carbon monoxide and other gases) from my body. I can now produce tears, but why should I cry? All I've experienced is your love and the care of my Creator.

My eyes move from side to side and can follow a light. I may even extend my hand to touch the light source. My head continues to grow to make room for my rapidly growing brain. My lanugo begins to disappear. I amuse myself by opening and closing my eyes and doing acrobatics. I say again, I am an Olympic champion; I am a beauty and a genius. Don't stop talking to me, praying for me, singing the special lullaby you wrote for me, and from reading my favorite story.

Prayer Guide for the Physical Development of Our Baby

Father, your existence is unequaled. You are who you are, the great I AM, and your greatness keeps amazing us. We thank you because your ways are perfect; your Word purifies and is a shield to those who wait upon you.

We declare your Word upon the bone marrow of our baby; we bless it with the ability to produce the red blood cells that carry oxygen and remove waste from the body.

We believe you, the great I AM, is in the midst of our baby, you save him, you enjoy and rejoice over him with songs of love. You have destroyed the power of death which could have tried to approach our baby.

As the great I AM, anoint his head with oil, watch over the growth of it and pour your anointment over his brain. We ask you to speak to his heart and that the words we speak to him and pray for him would be recorded in his heart and memory. We know all Scripture is inspired by God and profitable for teaching, for reproof, for correction and for training in righteousness and that is way we have prayed your Word over our baby. In the name of Jesus, we pray. Amen!

Prayer Guide for the Soul of Our Baby (emotions – mind – will)

And God said to Moses "I AM WHO I AM" and added: "You shall say to the sons of Israel: I AM has sent me to you. This is my name forever and with it my memory will be carried forever from generation to generation." You are our great I AM WHO I AM.

We trust that since your Word does everything for which it is sent, it is establishing itself in our baby's heart. The words of your mouth are pleasant to him and his heart's thoughts are already before you, oh LORD, our Rock, and our Redeemer. We prophesy your Word will be more desirable to him than gold, yes, more than fine gold and sweeter than honey distilled from the honeycomb. There will be a pure fear in his heart which will remain forever. He will know that the judgments of the Lord are true; they are all righteous. Furthermore, he will be counseled by them, knowing there is great reward in keeping them.

We know he will not be able to discern his mistakes on his own. Therefore, we ask you to free him from those that are hidden from his consciousness. Keep him from the sin of pride, so it will not have dominion over him so that he will be upright and innocent from transgression.

Beloved God, we prophesy faithfulness, fruit of the Holy Spirit, is part of our baby's genetics and he will remain faithful to your statutes. As he walks through life, his deeds will be bold and faithful, like the ones of Jehosheba, the daughter of Joram, who risked her life to save the life of the king's son, and hid him in her bedroom to preserve his life. In the name of Jesus, we pray. Amen!

Prayer Guide for the Spirit of Our Baby

Baby, once again, listen with your spirit to the Word of God for your life. Until now, all of your spiritual armor has been for protection and every one of them is important. This week we want to present you with the part of the armor used to directly attack the enemy of the souls. Listen with your spirit to the Word of God: "Take the helmet of salvation and the sword of the spirit, which is the Word of God." Dear baby, we pray the Word of God we are praying over you comes to life in your spirit and is engraved in your mind and in your heart. Baby, the Word of God is alive and effective and sharper than a two-edged sword; it pierces to the division of soul and spirit, to the joints and the bone marrow, and is powerful to discern the thoughts and intentions of the heart. It is the only weapon that has the power to defeat your enemy, Satan.

We prophesy you will love the Word of God and will not walk in the counsel of the wicked; you will not stand in the path of sinners, nor sit in the seat of those who do not give honor to the LORD; but in the law of the LORD will be your delight, and in his law you will meditate day and night.

We decree you will feel profound indignation because of the wicked that forsake God's law. At night you will remember the name of your LORD and you will rise up at midnight to thank God for his righteous ordinances. You will hasten and not delay to keep his commandments. You will be a companion to all those who fear him and keep his commandments. In the name of Jesus, we pray. Amen!

Eighth Month

Weeks 31-35

Summary of the Pregnancy Process

Week 31:   The rhythm of physical growth slows down; baby continues to gain weight. The brain enters a new rhythm of growth, producing hundreds of billions of new nerve cells.

Week 32:   The five senses are already functioning. The toenails are completely formed.

Week 33:   The size of the head has increased 3/8 of an inch due to the rapid growth of the brain. If it's a boy, the testicles continue to descend to the scrotum.

Week 34:   The baby has its own routine of sleeping and waking and has begun to blink. The baby may have already assumed a head down position.

Week 35:   The majority of babies born during this week can survive without any major problems. Hearing is completely developed. If it's a boy, his testicles have completed the descent process.

The Prayer Focus Will Be:

Week	Name of God	Bible Character	Prayer Focus The Soul	Prayer Focus The Spirit
31.	The Rock	Jesus	Fruit of Humbleness	Prayer
32.	Holy One of Israel	Samuel	Fruit of Humbleness	Present the gifts of the Holy Spirit: Gift of Wisdom
33.	Eternal God	Moses	Fruit of Humbleness	Gift of Knowledge
34.	Sun of Righteousness	John the Baptist	Fruit of Humbleness	Gift of Faith
35.	God that does Miracles	Joseph, Mary's husband	Fruit of Humbleness	Gift of Healing

The Festivals of Israel and Pregnancy

The Festivals of Israel	Pregnancy
N/A	N/A

Week 31: I am alive and I describe my development. I measure approximately 16.2 inches (41.1 cm) long and weigh about 3.3 lbs (1,502 g).

The Rock of Israel has made me grow. My physical growth rate slows down now and I won't grow much larger. I will gain a lot of weight as fat continues to accumulate. This layer of fat gives my skin the beautiful color I will have when I am born. I am also accumulating calcium, phosphorus and iron; my bones are growing and hardening.

My brain has entered a new period of rapid growth, producing hundreds of billions of new nerve cells. It's amazing! I may even move to the rhythm of music and show preference for a particular type of music over another. At this tender age, I am capable of dancing for my Creator. I am truly his masterpiece.

I produce several cups of urine daily into the amniotic fluid. Can you imagine what it would be like if you had to think about diapers? I am also swallowing amniotic fluid which majestically regenerates itself various times a day, just as the glory of God is always new.

My lungs are the only major organ yet to complete its development. I know you're eager to hold me in your arms. However, it is necessary for me to stay in my little house a little longer, for each day I stay in here improves my chances of breathing on my own outside of my Mommy's uterus.

Prayer Guide for the Physical Development of Our Baby

Beloved God, we ask that as the Rock of Israel has remained firm, may our baby remain firm in his mother's womb, growing and being comforted by the Holy Spirit, until the day of his birth. We believe the Holy Spirit of God fills him with wisdom and God's grace is upon him. We ask you to give him bones that are as strong as steel, and his extremities like iron bars.

We prophesy our baby will be a worshiper of God from his early childhood; he will rejoice in dancing for you, together with the young and the old. Dear God, during this new rhythm of growth of his brain, we ask you to care for the hundreds of billions of nerve cells being produced. Allow each neurological connection of his brain to be interwoven with your unequal intelligence and creativity. We believe our baby is being instructed by you, the Rock of Israel, and you will multiply his peace, for yours is the counsel, the prudence, the intelligence and the power, oh Rock of Israel. You are the portion of our inheritance and our cup. You sustain the destiny of our baby and will make him know the precise moment to be born. You will make known to him the path of life outside of his mother's womb. Meanwhile, we will rejoice in your presence where there is fullness of joy and at your right hand there are delights forevermore. In the name of Jesus, we pray. Amen!

Prayer Guide for the Soul of Our Baby (emotions – mind – will)

You are our firm Rock and we know we can trust in your promises and claim them for our baby. Therefore, we ask you to bless him with humbleness, fruit of the Holy Spirit. As one chosen of God, holy and beloved, may he be clothed with tender compassion, kindness, humility, humbleness and patience, sustaining and forgiving others. If anyone has a complaint against him, just as Jesus forgave, he too will forgive. We ask that he have a good conscience; so that in which he is defamed, those who slander his good behavior in Christ will be put to shame. For it is better to suffer for doing good, if that is the will of God, then for doing evil.

May he learn from you, for you are gentle and humble of heart, so he can find rest for his soul. Permit him to live in a manner worthy of the calling to which he was called from his mother's womb, being diligent to preserve the unity of the Spirit in the bond of peace. May he sanctify Christ as Lord in his heart, always being prepared to present a defense before anyone who demands a reason for the hope that is in him, yet with gentleness and reverence. In the name of Jesus, we pray. Amen!

Prayer Guide for the Spirit of Our Baby

Baby, we direct our voices to your spirit in the name of Jesus Christ. What we will instill in you are spiritual truths that can only be understood by your spirit. We will now instruct you about another piece of the spiritual clothing God has for you. Baby, listen with your spirit to the Word of God for you: "With all prayer and petition pray at all times in the Spirit, and with this in view, be on the alert with all perseverance and petition for all the saints."

Baby, after salvation, prayer is the most wonderful thing God has given us. To pray is to talk with God. Sometimes you will talk to him with your thoughts or emotions, but the yearning of your parents is for you to learn to spiritually connect with God. To pray in the spirit is to link your spirit to the Spirit of God. It is when your spirit, in a mysterious way, begins to proclaim the will of God in heaven through your mouth. Baby, we prophesy your spirit will long for spiritual things; you will have the confidence in God of knowing that if you ask anything according to his will, he hears you. With this confidence, you will ask him about the things to come regarding his people.

Baby, we prophesy you are a living rock, built as a spiritual house for a holy priesthood to offer spiritual sacrifices acceptable to God through Jesus Christ. You will be an intercessor, spiritually connected to God; in accordance with his kindness, he will hear your voice and quicken you according to his ordinances. We prophesy you will have your own prayer room. You will know and desire to close the door to your room and pray to your Father, who sees in secret, and he who sees in secret will reward you in public. Your private and public prayers will be prayers in the spirit, which will not depend on meaningless repetitions. They will be prayers so powerful that they will fill the place where you are praying and make the fire and glory of the LORD descend. They will cause everyone to prostrate their faces to the ground to worship and praise the LORD saying: "Truly, He is good; truly His loving kindness is everlasting." In the name of Jesus, we pray this over you. Amen!

Week 32: I am alive and I describe my development. I measure approximately 16.7 inches (42.4 cm) long and weigh about 3.75 lbs (1,702 g).

This week, I join my voice to yours to sing praises to the Holy One of Israel who gives me my final touches. I have grown so much since my conception, and continue to grow as I gain weight. My toenails are now completely formed and my hair continues to grow. It seems to me that you should be thinking of what stylist will give me my first haircut and pedicure. Meanwhile, I imagine that you must be wondering if I will have my father's or my mother's hair.

Mommy, you may have noticed that I no longer do as many acrobatics. Don't worry, I am fine; it's just that my little house seems to be getting smaller. I'm running out of space to move freely; but, I continue to practice my skills! My five senses are now working; I can smell, taste, hear, see and touch my surroundings. I am amazed with my five senses; I spend my time practicing how to use them as much as possible.

Prayer Guide for the Physical Development of Our Baby

We join our voices with the voice of our baby to sing praises to the Holy One of Israel. Just as Moses and the sons of Israel sang this song to the LORD and said: "I will sing to the LORD, for he is highly exalted; the horse and its rider he has tossed into the sea." Dear LORD, we thank you for the final touches you are giving to our baby, for the beauty and charm you have deposited in him.

We declare that his five physical senses will function perfectly, because they have been under the supervision of the Holy One of Israel. We ask for his beauty to be like the dawn, like a full moon, shining brightly as the sun and imposing as an army with banners.

We prophesy that if our baby is a boy, he will hold his head high, like Mount Carmel, and his hair will be like threads of brilliant purple. His eyes will be as the eyes of doves by currents of waters, washed with milk, and placed in their setting. His cheeks will be like a bed of spices, as sweet flowers, and his lips like lilies dropping sweet smelling myrrh. His hands will be like rods of gold set with beryl; his abdomen like carved ivory inlaid with sapphires. His legs will be like pillars of alabaster, set on pedestals of pure gold; his appearance will be like Lebanon, gallant as the cedars. His mouth will be full of sweetness and he will be all together lovely. This is how our baby will be, if it is a boy.

If it's a girl, her eyes will be like doves behind a veil; her hair like strands of pure silk. Her teeth will be like twin pearls. Her lips will be like a scarlet thread and her mouth lovely. Her cheeks will be like slices of pomegranate behind a veil. Her neck like the tower of David, built with rows of stones; her breasts will be like two fawns, twins of a gazelle, which walk among the lilies. The curve of her hips will be like jewels, the work of the hands of an artisan; her belly button will be like a round goblet, her belly like a heap of wheat surrounded by lilies.

Beloved Holy One of Israel, we are grateful that, up to now, you have kept the life of our baby and not allowed it to be born before its time. We know you will show our baby the precise time to be born. In the name of Jesus, we pray. Amen!

Prayer Guide for the Soul of Our Baby (emotions – mind – will)

Beloved Redeemer, our hearts' desire is that you sanctify the soul of our baby while it is still in its mother's womb. We ask you to plant in its heart the seed of humbleness, fruit of the Holy Spirit, make it flourish and produce much fruit. We're not asking this based on our own merits, but on the merits of your beloved son, Jesus Christ, in whom we have freedom and access to you with confidence through faith in him. Create in our baby, oh God, a clean heart filled with humbleness and firmness in you, like Samuel's, who was firm in your statutes in spite of being surrounded by bad examples.

We ask you to examine each thought that comes into his heart and cleanse them with hyssop. Allow his emotions to be subject to your precepts and free him from blood offenses. We prophesy our baby will grow under your shadow and as Samuel, will sing praises to you with all his soul, even in front of the gods of this earth. Open his lips, oh LORD, so his mouth will be able to proclaim your praises and from his childhood be able to hear your voice as Samuel heard you. May all his will and trust be subject to you and not to man; for your Word establishes that cursed be the man who trusts in man and makes the flesh his strength and his heart strays from the LORD. We ask you to keep his soul; do not allow it to become vain with human reasoning. Allow him to know you intimately and personally, so that his will is subject to you. Keep his mind from the ignorance and vanity of the world he will be living in. Do not allow his understanding to be darkened or insensitivity and sensuality to overpower our baby and harden his heart. In the name of Jesus, we pray. Amen!

Prayer Guide for the Spirit of Our Baby

Spirit of our baby, we speak to you in the name of Jesus Christ. Listen carefully to each word spoken to you because, we are going to feed your spirit. Listen with your spirit to what the Word of God says: "Brothers, I don't want you to be ignorant about the spiritual gifts." Beloved baby, the desire of God's heart is that you know him. God wants you to take possession of all the gifts the Holy Spirit. There is a lot to teach you about the gifts that are available to you. Spirit of our baby, rejoice in hearing what God tells you in his Word about the gifts of the Spirit. "Now there are diversity of gifts, but the same Spirit." "But to each one is given the manifestation of the Spirit for the common good. For to one is given by the Spirit the word of wisdom; to another the word of knowledge by the same Spirit; to another faith by the same Spirit; to another the gifts of healing by the same Spirit; to another the effecting of miracles; to another, prophesy; to another the discerning of spirits; to another diverse kinds of tongues; to another the interpretation of tongues. But one and the same Spirit works all these things, distributing to each one individually just as he wishes."

Baby, the Bible not only tells us that the nine gifts are available for all believers, but adds that we should earnestly desire all the gifts, above all, the gift of prophecy. The Bible also teaches us not to quench the Spirit nor neglect our spiritual gift, but, on the contrary, we should kindle the fire of God's gift. Baby, in the name of Jesus, we prophesy that your spirit is quickened from your mother's womb and you are a vessel separated for God. The Holy Spirit will visit you and manifest the gift of wisdom upon your life; it shall be so intense that many will be amazed at your ability to comprehend supernatural things, and how you handle complex situations. In the name of Jesus, we pray. Amen!

Week 33: I am alive and I describe my development. I measure approximately 17.2 inches (43.7 cm) long and weigh about 4.23 lbs (1,918 g).

Do you not know? Have you not heard? The Everlasting God, The LORD, the Creator of the boundaries of the earth does not fatigue nor gets tired. In spite of the many things he is involved in, he has taken charge of my development. Truly, his understanding is inscrutable. He made sure the size of my head would increase 3/8 of an inch to adjust to the rapid growth of my brain. He assured that my neurons and synapses would develop into thousands of millions, forming new connections to provide me with the skills needed to survive outside of my Mommy's womb as a newborn baby. Wonderful are the works of my Creator! Perhaps this week, I may be able to coordinate sucking my thumb, swallowing and breathing. You will agree that I'm quite a genius.

While most of my bones are hardening, my skull is quite pliable and not completely joined. My bones will be able to move slightly to make birthing easier. I may already have periods of sleep where I dream. I know you're probably wondering what I dream about. This is a secret between my Creator and me. I continue to practice using my lungs because it prepares me for breathing outside the uterus. If I'm a boy, my testicles continue to descend to the scrotum. Sometimes one of the testicles will not move into position until after birth.

Prayer Guide for the Physical Development of Our Baby

Eternal God, how can we not exalt your name? You have taken care of every detail of the formation of our baby and our hearts overflow with joy and gratitude. Thank you for crowning his head with the exact measurements he has needed during his process of growth and development. We ask you to separate him for yourself and place your crown of holiness upon his head and brain in formation. While our baby is still in his mother's womb, may he be taught by you, Eternal God. Multiply his peace, for you have promised to multiply the peace of your sons.

Eternal God, you are the one who preserves man and beast. Your loving kindness extends to the heavens, your faithfulness reaches to the skies. We ask that, as our baby practices to swallow, suck his thumb, and breathe inside its mother's womb, you satisfy him with the abundance of your house. Give him to drink from the river of your delights, because in you is the fountain of life and in your light we see the light. Grant that just as with your rebuke and blast of the breath from your nostrils, the springs of the sea appeared and the foundation of the world was laid bare, the lungs and respiratory tract of our baby be blessed. If our baby is a boy, we ask you to take care of the path of his testicles on their descent to the scrotum. In the name of Jesus, we pray. Amen!

Prayer Guide for the Soul of Our Baby (emotions – mind – will)

We worship and bless you; you are the Eternal God, the LORD, and the creator of the boundaries of the earth. You do not get weary or tired. Your understanding is inscrutable. You give power to the faint and weary and might to him who lacks it. Even the young grow weary and tired, the children stumble and hesitate, but those who wait on the LORD will gain new strength. They will rise up with wings like eagles, they will run and not get tired, will walk and not become weary. We claim this promise for our baby and ask you to be his strength and saving defense. May our baby understand, as Moses did, that no one can be strong in his own might. You save your people and bless your inheritance and shepherd them forever.

Oh Eternal God, we declare that our baby is blessed, his strength is in you and his heart is in your path! We know that, in his life, there will be times when his humanity will want to reign and allow worldly images to take control of him. We ask that in those moments, meekness will beat much stronger in his heart with the conviction that no temptation will overtake him that is not common to man. Faithful is God who will not allow him to be tempted beyond what he can bear; but with the temptation God also provides a way of escape, so he will be able to endure it. In the name of Jesus, we pray. Amen!

Prayer Guide for the Spirit of Our Baby

Spirit of our baby, we speak to you in the name of Jesus Christ. Listen carefully to each word that we speak, because we want to continue feeding you with the Word of God. Listen with your spirit to what the Word of God says about the gifts of the Spirit: "For to one is given the word of wisdom through the Spirit; to another, the word of knowledge by the same Spirit." Baby, during this week we are going to speak to you about the gift of knowledge, for the Word of God teaches us that the people of God are destroyed because of the lack of knowledge. This has never been the will of God.

Our God is the Alpha and Omega, the beginning and the end; this means he is all knowing and nothing is hidden from him. We, your parents, declare that you will yearn for the gifts of the spirit. God will reveal to you the mysteries of the darkness and bring to light the deep darkness. He will reveal to you the thoughts of men and what will happen in the future. Baby, we prophesy your inheritance is in Jesus Christ, and you will be a servant of Christ and administrator of the mysteries of God. We prophesy you will be a friend of the Holy Spirit. Just as God did not hide from Abraham his plan of destroying Sodom, God will reveal his plans and mysteries concerning you and others. Baby, we bless you with the constant manifestation of supernatural knowledge that is beyond your own knowledge or human intelligence. In the name of Jesus, we pray. Amen!

**Week 34: I am alive and I describe my development.
I measure approximately 17.7 inches (45 cm)
long and weigh about 4.7 lbs (2,146 g).**

The Sun of Righteousness has shined. I now behave as a newborn baby with my eyes open when I'm awake and closed when I'm sleeping. I also have my own routine for sleeping and being awake. I have learned to blink my beautiful eyes. My fingernails have grown to the tips of my fingers. Perhaps I'll have even scratched my face before I am born. Definitely, it's time to make an appointment for my first manicure!

The Sun of Righteousness has shined upon me and has flooded me with his love. I can see more clearly when there is light on Mommy's tummy. I probably have the outline of all her organs memorized! What I definitely have engraved in my mind and heart are the feelings of love and acceptance you have expressed to me. The reflection of your love is so clear that I don't need any other external source to perceive how much I am loved and wanted.

Mommy's antibodies are transferred to me through her blood and will continue to protect me until my birth. Later, my Mommy's breast milk will provide the nutrients I need to protect me against diseases. Only my God could have thought of an immune system like this one. He also gave me my own biological clock. I may have already assumed a head-down position in preparation for that great day when I'll leave my little house to be deposited in your loving arms.

Prayer Guide for the Physical Development of Our Baby

The Sun of Righteousness has shined on our baby and the glory of God has crowned him. Our baby is like a royal crown in the hands of our God. Dear LORD, we thank you for opening his eyes; we pray you would allow your precepts to delight his heart and illuminate his eyes. Father, we know it was customary for Moses to have his tent meetings outside the camp and everyone who sought the Lord would go there. We ask that our baby, from the womb, establish the habit of spending long periods of time alone in your presence, speaking with you as with a friend. May every word of the Scriptures we have prayed over him be engraved in his heart and mind.

We worship you, for as sun and shield is the immune system you have provided for our baby. We declare no sickness will pierce him, for you do not deny anything good to your sons. Thank you, Sun of Righteousness, for the blessing of his mother's breasts. We are amazed by the miracle of how our baby can be fed and protected by the maternal milk. Its contents will continue to protect him, and at the same time help establish a bonding relationship that makes him feel confident from his mother's breasts.

As the time of his birth approaches, may you, the Sun of Righteousness shine upon our baby, call him by his name, hold his hand and position him correctly for his birth. We know the exact day and time of his birth belongs to your secret things. As we don't know how clouds are positioned or the wonders of your perfect knowledge, we are unaware of the exact day or time of our baby's birth. Moreover, we know when the exact time comes, you will give our baby the signal that it is time for him to be delivered into our arms and your powerful hand will guide him down the birth canal. In the name of Jesus, we pray. Amen!

Prayer Guide for the Soul of Our Baby (emotions – mind – will)

You are our Sun of Righteousness. To you we lift up our voices and ask that from his mother's womb, our baby's soul would passionately desire to come into your presence, and his heart and flesh sing to the God of Righteousness. May he forever enjoy the blessing of dwelling in your presence and praising you.

We prophesy his strength will be in you, and his heart fixed in your ways, so when he crosses dry valleys he turns them into streams of water, like rain that fills the fountains. We ask that he fear your name and your Sun of Righteousness shine upon him with health.

LORD, hear our prayer; listen oh God; look, our shield, set your eyes upon our baby and guard his heart. Enlighten the eyes of his heart so he will understand his identity in you and delight in it as John the Baptist did, who understood his role was to announce the coming of the Messiah, proclaiming: "I am not the Christ, but I have been sent ahead of Him." He prophesied that he would decrease while Jesus would increase in his ministry. We ask that the spirit of meekness reign in the heart of our baby all the years of his life, for your Word establishes that blessed are the meek, for they shall inherit the earth. In the name of Jesus, we pray. Amen!

Prayer Guide for the Spirit of Our Baby

Beloved Baby, in the name of Jesus Christ, we call your spirit to attention. Listen to what the Word of God says about another gift of the Holy Spirit. "For to one is given the word of wisdom by the Spirit; to another, the word of knowledge according to the same Spirit; to another, faith by the same Spirit." Today, we'll be teaching you about the gift of faith that comes directly from the Spirit. The Word of God teaches us that "Without faith it is impossible to please Him, for he who comes to God must believe that He is and that He is a rewarder of those who seek Him." It also states that every one of us has received a measure of faith; God will never ask us for anything for which he has not already made provision. Faith, as a gift, is supernatural; it is a manifestation of the extraordinary power of God that brings man to believe in supernatural things. This gift works in conjunction with other gifts, such as the gift of performing miracles or the gifts of healing.

Baby, the gift of faith is a gift from your Helper, the Holy Spirit. The manifestation of this gift will help you leave your comfort zone and dare you to move to a supernatural level. Baby, we your parents bless you with a fervent desire to manifest the glory of God, through the gift of faith. We declare your faith will enable you to even order a mountain to move and it will move. Nothing will be impossible to you, provided that when you ask for it, it is aligned with the Word of God.

We prophesy you will speak the Word of God, not with persuasive words of human wisdom, but in demonstration of the Spirit and of power, thanks to the manifestation of the gift of faith. For your faith does not rest on the wisdom of men, but on the power of God. In the name of Jesus, we pray. Amen!

Week 35: I am alive and I describe my development.
I measure approximately 18.2 inches (46.2 cm)
long and weigh about 5.25 lbs (2,383 g).

The God who performs miracles has allowed that during this week, a period of rapid increase in weight begins of approximately 8 to 12 ounces a week. Relax, you won't have to put me on a diet. These are layers of fat my Creator gives me to help regulate my body temperature. They also make me beautiful, because they form those cute dimples in my elbows and knees. If I'm a boy, my testicles have completed their descent. My hearing is fully developed. Don't stop speaking and praying for me; I enjoy listening to your voices.

I already occupy all the space in my little house. Sometimes when I stretch out, I pressure Mommy's diaphragm and lungs and she has to make an extra effort to breath. I'm sorry Mommy; I do not want to harm you; but don't worry, very soon I will position myself in your pelvis. You'll then be able to breathe a little better, although you may not be able to walk so easily. Patience, there's just a little time left for my arrival. I assure you that when you see me you'll forget all about these discomforts.

Prayer Guide for the Physical Development of Our Baby

You are the God who works miracles and our souls know it very well. We love you with all our hearts, our souls and our strength. We believe you have heard our prayers and we thank you for the growth and development of our baby. Thank you for making him beautiful during this week and for assuring that he has the necessary layers of fat to regulate his temperature.

LORD, we trust you have cared for our baby's hearing and the Word we have prayed over him resides in his heart and mind with abundance of wisdom and brings him happiness and joy. We thank you for keeping him and guiding him toward the birth canal. In the name of Jesus, Christ we pray. Amen!

Prayer Guide for the Soul of Our Baby
(emotions – mind – will)

You are the God who works miracles! We have known your strength among the people and have seen the miracles you continue to do. We bow before you and give thanks to your name, for your mercy and faithfulness, because you have magnified your Word according to your name. Father, in a miraculous way, our baby already hears our voices; we know every word we have prayed over him is being engraved in all of his being. We ask you to also open his ears to instruction; plant the seed of meekness and wisdom in his innermost being and give intelligence to his mind. Allow him to demonstrate the meekness Joseph exhibited when he found out that Mary, to whom he was engaged, was pregnant.

We pray our baby's personality will reflect the fruit of meekness and he will not think more highly of himself than he ought to think. We ask for wisdom to enter his heart, knowledge to be pleasant to his soul, the ability to discern justice and judgment, equity and every good path. We prophesy that just like Joseph, discretion will guard him, understanding will watch over him to deliver him from the way of evil, from the man who speaks perverse things and from those who leave the paths of the righteous to walk in the ways of darkness. He will set his eyes on the things above, not on the things of this earth. In the name of Jesus, we pray. Amen!

Prayer Guide for the Spirit of Our Baby

Our very beloved baby, in the name of Jesus Christ, we now speak to your spirit. Listen carefully while we teach you about the gifts of healing. Listen with your spirit to what the Word of God says: "But to each one is given the manifestation of the Spirit for the common good. For to one is given the word of wisdom by the Spirit; to another the word of knowledge according to the same Spirit; to another faith by the same Spirit, to another the gifts of healing by the same Spirit." Baby, the first thing we want you to notice is that the Bible talks about gifts of healing, not just one healing gift. This means there are many gifts of healing.

Baby, as we've been repeating over and over again, God loves us. In ancient times, God the Father presented himself as Jehovah Rapha, our healer, he who brings health and healing. In the New Testament we find Jesus healing and liberating the captives. He also sent his disciples to put their hands upon the sick and heal them. Later, through the power of the person of the Holy Spirit, the gifts continued to be manifested, regularly and frequently, by the disciples.

Baby, without a doubt, the desire of the heart of God is to anoint his sons with the gifts of healing. Our appeal to God has been that from your mother's womb, all your being, spirit, soul and body be covered by the healing power of Jehovah Rapha, and the manifestation of the gifts of healing would be infused in your spirit and become part of your spiritual genetics.

We prophesy you will be a vessel of his healing power. The anointing of the gifts of healing will be so strong upon you, that in fact, people will take handkerchiefs or aprons from your body to the sick. Their illness will leave them, regardless of the type of disease or the doctor's diagnosis, and the evil spirits will come out of them. In the name of Jesus, we pray. Amen!

Ninth Month

Weeks 36-40

Summary of the Pregnancy Process

Week 36: The only organ still in the process of maturing are the lungs.

Week 37: Baby has already reached its term and is ready to be born. Baby continues to practice breathing.

Week 38: Baby gets a lot of hiccups as a result of the lack of air due to the many breathing exercise it does. The intestines are functioning.

Week 39: The lungs continue to develop up to the moment of birth.

Week 40: Baby is ready to be born. Day of birth.

The Prayer Focus Will Be:

Week	Name of God	Bible Character	Prayer Focus The Soul	Prayer Focus The Spirit
36.	Our Redeemer	David	Fruit of Self-Control	Gift of Miracles
37.	LORD of LORDS	Timothy	Fruit of Self-Control	Gift of Prophecy
38.	Arm of The LORD	Lot	Fruit of Self-Control	Gift of Discernment of Spirits
39.	The LORD is Present	Joseph, son of Jacob	Fruit of Self-Control	Various Kinds of Tongues Interpretation of Tongues
40.	Power of My Salvation	Shadrach, Meshach and Abed-nego	Self-Control	Consecrated from the Womb
Birth	Alpha and Omega	N/A	N/A	N/A

The Festivals of Israel and Pregnancy

The Festivals of Israel	Pregnancy
Feast of Dedication Also known as the festival of lights. According to the Jewish calendar, the time between the Feast of Tabernacles and the Feast of Dedication begins on the 280th day. The feast lasts eight days.	**Birth of Baby** The doctors calculate the pregnancy on the basis of 280 days. The birth can happen between the 40th and the 42nd week.

Week 36: I am alive and I describe my development. I measure approximately 18.66 inches (47.4 cm) long and weigh about 5.78 lbs (2,622 g).

The LORD, my Savior, my Redeemer, the Almighty of Jacob has taken care of us. It seems I'm almost ready for my triumphant entrance into your arms, my beloved parents, who have covered me with your love and prayers. All of my being perceives how much you love me and want me in your arms. Patience, because the longer I stay in my little house, the greater the probability I have of breathing on my own, since the only organ still in the process of maturing are my lungs.

My skin continues to gather fat and is becoming softer, looking more like that of a baby. I am beautiful; the wrinkles have disappeared. Glory to my God! I praise him because he has made everything beautiful in its time. I have accumulated fat on my cheeks and I look stunning. Pretty soon your hands will be able to caress them and give me lots of tender kisses. How I long for that day to come!

Mommy, please be careful with what you eat at this stage. I'm gaining weight, about one ounce per day. We don't want to need a personal trainer. My kidneys are completely developed; and my liver has begun to process waste. If I haven't done so yet, this week I will position myself inside your pelvis. The bones that form my skull can move relative to one another. They overlap each other so my head is able to comfortably fit inside Mommy's pelvis. My Creator designed this wonder so my head can make its way through the birth canal. Don't be surprised if at birth my head looks pointed or misshapen; my Creator took care of that and after a couple of hours or days it will regain the round shape again.

Prayer Guide for the Physical Development of Our Baby

The LORD, our Savior, Redeemer, the Mighty One of Jacob is the one in whom we have trusted. For you are our rock and fortress; by your name you will guide and bring our baby into our arms.

We know that the soul of all life and the spirit of all human flesh are in your hands. Thank you for guarding and covering his: kidneys, liver and lungs while our baby is still in his mother's womb. From his conception, you have molded him like clay. You poured out, like milk, what was necessary for every organ to be formed and then you curdled them like cheese. You dressed him with skin and flesh and knit him with bones and tendons. You granted him life and mercy and your care has guarded his spirit. You have girded him with strength and made perfect his way, assuring he positions himself in his mother's pelvis to make his way through the birth canal on the day and hour that you have destined for his birth. In the name of Jesus, we pray. Amen!

Prayer Guide for the Soul of Our Baby (emotions – mind – will)

Powerful are you, our LORD and Redeemer. We will worship only you, for your fidelity is forever. Almighty God, we know there is nothing too difficult for you. You listen to the desires of the humble, strengthen their hearts, and incline your ear to their petitions. With this confidence, we ask you to deposit the seed of self-control, fruit of the Holy Spirit, into the soul of our baby.

Allow him to know how to patiently wait upon you. Help him recognize that his times are in your hands; and his will is subject to your will. May he wait on you as David did, who in spite of knowing he was chosen as king, did not rush to take matters into his own hands, but showed a reverent fear for your principles and waited upon you. May he trust you, do what is good and cultivate faithfulness. May you be his delight and he entrust his way unto you.

We prophesy our baby will recognize that man's steps are ordained by Jehovah and it is he who approves them. Our child will entrust his way to you, Oh LORD. He will wait upon you in silence with the conviction that as you did with David, you will exalt him in your time. You will make his righteousness shine as a light and your cause as the midday light.

Your law will be in his heart and his steps will not vacillate; they will make him trust silently in the Lord and wait with patience. He will not fret because of those that prosper or by the man who carries out wicked schemes, but will open his lips to declare your praises. He will rejoice in the way of your testimonies more than all of the riches of the world. In the name of Jesus, we pray. Amen!

Prayer Guide for the Spirit of Our Baby

Baby, we call your spirit to attention, in the name of Jesus Christ, listen with your spirit to what the Word of God says to you: "But the manifestation of the Spirit is given to every man to profit all. For to one is given by the Spirit the word of wisdom; to another the word of knowledge by the same Spirit; to another the working of miracles."

Spirit of our baby, this week we will instruct you on the gift of miracles. By miracles we understand that it's a phenomenon that transcends natural laws or a divine act in which God reveals himself. The performing of miracles is God's daily tasks. The very creation of the world is a miracle, where God spoke the word and what he spoke was created. He divided the Red Sea so his people would cross on dry land; he closed the mouth of lions so no harm would be done to his servant Daniel. He made the fingers of a human hand appear and write on a wall, converted water into wine and fed 5,000 people with 5 loaves of bread and 2 fish. Baby, what we just mentioned are just a few of the many miracles described in the Bible.

The Word of God teaches us that Jesus is the same yesterday, today, and forever. Whoever believes in him will not only do the deeds he has done, but even greater ones. Spirit of our baby, we remind you that you must ask for these gifts.

We prophesy your spirit is quickened within you; you will desire the gifts from the Spirit. You will delight yourself in the LORD. The testimony of Christ will be confirmed in you and you will know the thoughts of God for you. As the deer pants for the streams of water, so you will ardently cry out with all your being for the spiritual gifts. You will do miracles and wonders. In the name of Jesus, we pray. Amen!

Week 37: I am alive and I describe my development. I measure approximately 19.1 inches (48.6 cm) long and weigh about 6.3 lbs (2,859 g).

The LORD of Lords is a great God, powerful and awesome. His powerful hand has protected me and I'm ready to leave my little house; but, I can still stay a little longer. I haven't stopped growing. I will continue developing fat at the rate of half an ounce per day. I hope I can fit into the clothes you have bought for me.

I now have a firm grasp and soon I'll use it to firmly grab Mommy's and Daddy's fingers. I continue to practice breathing movements. It's a miracle what my Creator has done. He make it possible for me to be able breathe underwater.

I can now, not only, turn my eyes toward the light coming from the outside, but I can also turn myself toward it. As Mommy's skin stretches and becomes thinner, more light reaches me. I know my Creator lives and is the true light that came to the world and illuminates all of mankind.

Mommy, remember that this is a good time to establish a pattern for resting for both of us. Have you ever heard it said that the baby has mixed up his days and nights? Now is the time to avoid this, establishing a fixed time for rest.

Prayer Guide for the Physical Development of Our Baby

We magnify you because you are the LORD our God, Lord of lords, great God, powerful and awesome, that does not show partiality toward persons nor takes bribes. By your mercy, you gave yourself as a shield of health; your right hand sustains our baby. In your right hand you bring him long life, in your left hand riches and honor.

We thank you for having cared for our baby's lungs, for miraculously allowing our baby to breathe inside the amniotic fluid surrounding him. We trust that you, who are eyes to the blind and feet to the lame and do everything perfect, will show our baby the precise moment of his birth. In the meantime, help us to be wise in establishing a routine that would edify the life of our baby in spirit, soul and body. In the name of Jesus, we pray. Amen!

Prayer Guide for the Soul of Our Baby (emotions – mind – will)

You are our LORD, King of kings, Lord of lords, great, powerful and awesome God, who shows no partiality of persons. Admirable are your deeds in favor of the sons of men. You have provided your shield of salvation for our baby; your right hand upholds him and your benevolence magnifies him.

LORD, our heart's desire for our baby is that he be set apart from the womb for you, and by your grace you call him and direct his steps. As you revealed yourself to Timothy in his infancy, may Christ, your beloved son, be revealed to our child so his feet would hold fast to your path and not turn away from it.

LORD, we know you are the one who works in us the desire, as well as the doing of your will, for your pleasure. Therefore, we ask you to help our baby to seek you with all his heart, and as a result of his search, self-control reign in his soul.

We prophesy he will not depart from your commandments. His heart will treasure your Word, so he may not sin against you. Blessed are you, Oh LORD. Teach him your statutes, to meditate on your precepts and regard your ways. May he delight in your statutes and not forget your Word.

Beloved God, show favor toward our baby so he may live and desire to keep your Word. Open his eyes so he may see the wonderful things from your law and understand that his travel on earth is just a pilgrimage. Cause his soul to breakout with longing for your ordinances at all times. In the name of Jesus, we pray. Amen!

Prayer Guide for the Spirit of Our Baby

Baby, we direct our voices to your spirit in the name of Jesus Christ. Listen with your spirit to what the Word of God says about you: "But the manifestation of the Spirit is given to every man to profit all. For to one is given by the Spirit the word of wisdom; to another the word of knowledge by the same Spirit; to another the working of miracles; to another prophecy."

Baby, this week we'll be teaching you about the gift of prophesy. To prophesy is to receive a word directly from the heart of the LORD. It is an act of proclaiming to someone a message on behalf of the Spirit of God. A prophetic word is not based on your intellect, rather on the gift of God. The word given under the gift of prophecy will always be for the edification, exhortation and consolation of the person to whom it is given. The prophetic word will confirm what God has already told the person.

Beloved baby, the very Word of God teaches us that this is a gift that, above all the rest, you should earnestly seek. Therefore, in the name of Jesus, we your parents declare that the word we have prayed over you does everything for which it is sent. You will incline your spiritual ear to these words and as you grow and develop, the Holy Spirit will remind you of everything you have been taught. Your spirit will desire the gift of prophesy for the common good of the church. Baby, God has qualified you to share in the inheritance of the saints and He will pour out his spirit upon you and you will prophesy. In the name of Jesus, we pray. Amen!

**Week 38: I am alive and I describe my development.
I measure approximately 19.6 inches (49.8 cm)
long and weigh about 6.8 lbs (3,083 g).**

The arm of the LORD has been revealed. He has made me beautiful and will guide me to the arms of my beloved parents.

The circumference of my head and my abdomen measure about the same. My head may be fully covered with hair. I imagine you continue wondering about the color and texture of my hair. If I'm a boy, my testicles have descended to my scrotum. If I'm a girl, my vaginal lips are completely formed. My intestines are working and accumulating meconium, my first potty. I hope you're ready with my diapers.

You may have noticed that I get a lot of hiccups. The reason for this is that I am a champion swimming underwater; as a result of the lack of air around me, my breathing exercise causes amniotic fluid to enter my windpipe and I get the hiccups.

Prayer Guide for the Physical Development of Our Baby

The arm of our LORD has been revealed. He has made our baby beautiful and will guide him to our arms. We know our LORD, therefore, we are sure the precise moment of our baby's arrival is as certain as the dawn. He will come to us as the rain, as the spring rain that waters the land.

Our hearts are overjoyed, for we know the one who guards our baby will not sleep nor slumber. The LORD is his keeper; the LORD is his shade on his right hand. The LORD will protect him from all evil; He will keep his soul. The LORD's arm will guard his exit and entrance from this time forth and forever. Even the hair on his head has been counted by our God. The help of our baby comes from the arm of the LORD, who made heaven and earth and will not allow his foot to slip; he who guards our baby will not slumber. In the name of Jesus, we pray. Amen!

Prayer Guide for the Soul of Our Baby (emotions – mind – will)

The arm of the LORD has clothed itself with power, as in ancient times, it has unveiled itself to us. By the power of your arm you have done wonders. We will forever exalt your name and exalt you for the wonderful way you have cared for our baby. You have protected him and kept him alive.

Father, we ask that as your hand has upheld him and physically guarded him, that you would also guard his heart. Give him an understanding heart to discern between good and evil. We know he will live in a world where sin is exceedingly grievous, where like Sodom and Gomorrah, the expressions on the faces of the people bear witness against them. People display their sin; they do not conceal it and have brought evil upon themselves.

We know our baby will need more from you than any other generation. In light of this reality, we ask for the seed of self-control, fruit of the Holy Spirit, to be firmly rooted in his heart. Just as the deer pants for the streams of water, may his soul yearn for you. May he earnestly seek you, because his soul thirsts for you; like a dry and weary land where there is no water.

We ask that at a very early age you would convict our child of sin, of justice and judgment. To you we entrust our child; for you know how to rescue the godly from temptation, and to keep the unrighteous under punishment for the Day of Judgment. Father, rescue him like you rescued righteous Lot, who was oppressed by the sensual conduct of unprincipled men. May his righteous soul feel repulsed by lawless deeds, and on the contrary, may his soul long for and yearn for the courts of the LORD. May his heart and flesh sing for joy to the living God. In the name of Jesus, we pray. Amen!

Prayer Guide for the Spirit of Our Baby

Spirit of our baby, we speak to you in the name of Jesus Christ. Listen carefully to each word we'll be speaking to you. We want to feed you with the Word of God and teach you about the gifts of the Spirit. Listen with your spirit to what the Word of God tells you: "But the manifestation of the Spirit is given to every man to profit all. For to one is given by the Spirit the word of wisdom; to another the word of knowledge by the same Spirit; to another the working of miracles; to another prophecy; to another discerning of spirits."

Baby, the gift of the discerning of spirits refers to the supernatural power to detect the world of demonic spirits, angelical spirits or human spirits, and to know their activities. It's when the Spirit of God gives you a vision or spiritual knowledge to know supernaturally, the plans of the enemy, the divine intervention of God or the true spirit that could be operating in a person.

Baby, this gift is needed very much at this time when demonic activity is increasing; but be confident, for the Word of God establishes that where sin abounds, grace abounds all the more. We your parents bless you with the earnest desire to flow in the spiritual gifts. We bless you with the gift of discerning between the deceiving spirits of darkness, the ministering angels of God, and the true nature of the spirit of the people who approach you. Baby, we bless you with a vision that goes beyond the physical world to penetrate the spiritual world, in order to unmask the enemy of souls.

We prophesy your spiritual eyes will be equipped to be a successful leader, who will see how the angels of God are working in your favor and in the favor of others. No human spirit will deceive you. Rather, you will know how to discern between the righteous and the wicked, between one who serves God, and the one who does not serve him. You will live a victorious life in Christ Jesus. In the name of Jesus, we pray. Amen!

***Week 39: I am alive and I describe my development.
I measure approximately 19.9 inches (50.7 cm)
long and weigh about 7.25 lbs (3,288 g).***

The LORD is present! The spirit of God made me and the inspiration of the Almighty gave me life. My lungs are mature and I'm ready for my trip into the loving arms of my parents. As I prepare for my trip to the exterior, most of the lanugo and the special moisturizing cream my Creator patented, called vernix, has disappeared. Perhaps there is a little left on my back and other parts of my body. Mommy's placenta provides me with the antibodies that will help my immune system fight infection for the first six to twelve months of my life. I don't have much room left to move around in.

Mommy, you must agree that it's amazing how I can manage to pressure your ribs and bladder at the same time. I continue to store fat, which regulates my temperature. Beloved parents, there are just a couple of days left before you have me in your arms. I am at peace, for I am confident that he who began a good work in me, will perfect it. With this confidence, I enter into God's rest and I invite you to do the same.

Prayer Guide for the Physical Development of Our Baby

As the birth date approaches, it comforts us to know the LORD, our God, is here in our midst and watches for the fulfillment of his Word, which is alive, full of power and will do everything for which it is sent. LORD, we know you are here in our midst; your way is perfect and you are a shield to all who seek refuge in you. You are the one who listens when we invoke you and you let yourself be found by us. You hear us in whatever we ask and respond to our petitions. You have said to ask and it shall be given; seek and you shall find, knock and it shall be opened to you. Your Word establishes there is an appointed time for everything and a time for every event under heaven. We, therefore, know when the appointed time comes, you will indicate it. Your good word to us will be fulfilled. You will open the birth canal and our baby will be born; and we will see the fruit of our hope. Until that moment arrives, we enter into your rest. Our God is here, caring for our baby. In his hand is the soul of all living being and the spirit of all human flesh.

You have guarded and conserved the life of our baby. Our hearts are glad, our souls rejoice and our flesh will dwell in safety, for you are Our Rock and Our Fortress. For the love of your name, you will lead our baby to our arms. You are the one who keeps him alive and does not allow his feet to slip; you will protect him from all evil. This is our confidence! When anxiety tries to seize us, we will cast all of our anxiety on you, for we know you care for us. In the name of Jesus, we pray. Amen!

Prayer Guide for the Soul of Our Baby (emotions – mind – will)

Dear LORD, thank you for always being here for us, for dwelling in our hearts and for caring for our baby. We ask you to cover him with your love. We remind you that we have placed him in your hands, with the conviction that you do not forsake the work of your hands, and your purpose will be fulfilled in his life. Allow our baby to stretch his hands out to you; may his soul long for you as a thirsty land. On the day he invokes you, answer him and strengthen his soul.

We know that periods of anguish will undoubtedly touch his life. In times of anguish, we ask you to revive him, stretch forth your hand against the wrath of his enemies, and your right hand save him. Upon seeing your salvation, may he meditate on all your works and reflect on all your deeds. At a very early age, may he comprehend that he must exercise self-control over the desires of his flesh and soul.

May he, with great determination, imitate the behavior of Joseph, Jacob's son, who resisted the sexual seductions of his master's wife. Create in him the conviction that his life belongs to you, with the certainty that those who belong to Jesus Christ have crucified the flesh with its passions and desires.

Incline his heart to your testimonies and not to dishonest gain. Turn his eyes away from vanity and revive him in your ways, so he understands that the eye is the lamp of the body; if his eye is clear, his whole body will be filled with light. Confirm your Word in our baby and inspire in him reverence for you. In the name of Jesus, we pray. Amen!

Prayer Guide for the Spirit of Our Baby

Our very beloved baby, in the name of Jesus Christ, we now speak to your spirit. Listen carefully to the Word of God for you; "For to one is given the word of wisdom through the Spirit, to another various kinds of tongues, and to another the interpretation of tongues."

Baby, this week we're going to teach you about the gift of various kinds of tongues and the interpretation of tongues, which are part of the signs Jesus said will accompany those who have believed in him. The gift of various kinds of tongues is when the Holy Spirit gives you the supernatural ability to speak in a language you do not have the ability or knowledge to speak. They can be human languages, languages that actually exist or dialects of ancient cultures. They can also be angelical languages. When one speaks in tongues, one does not speak to men but to God, for no one understands, but in your spirit you speak the mysteries of God.

This gift is very useful when we don't know how to pray. When praying in tongues, it is our spirit that intercedes for us with groanings too deep for words. Baby, the gift of interpretation of tongues comes to complement the gift of tongues. It allows you to understand what you or another person is saying. The Word of God teaches us that we should ask for the gift of interpretation for the benefit of our understanding. The interpretation of tongues is not a translation. Rather a declaration of the meaning of the tongues, because the one who interprets does not understand the language he is interpreting. It's a miraculous and supernatural phenomenon of the Holy Spirit.

Baby, these two gifts comprise part of the package of the gifts God has made available to all who want them. We your parents, in the name of Jesus, declare you will flow in speaking new human and angelical languages. You will have your own language to communicate with God. We prophesy your spirit joins with the spirit of God in prayers that touch the heart of God and take you to a new level of intimacy with him. We prophesy you will speak angelical languages of war that will strengthen you in the power of his might, while tearing down principalities, the rulers and powers of darkness of this century, and the spiritual forces of wickedness in the heavenly places.

Baby, in the name of Jesus, we bless you with the gift of the interpretation of tongues. We prophesy you are an ambassador of God and he who God has sent, speaks the words of God, for God gives the spirit without measure. Your spirit will cry out "Abba, Father!" You will long to discover the mysteries of God when you speak in tongues. In a supernatural way the Holy Spirit will give you, without measure, the gift of the interpretation of tongues. In the name of Jesus, we pray. Amen!

Week 40: I am alive and I describe my development. I measure approximately 20.2 inches (51.2 cm) long and weigh about 7.6 lbs (3,462 g).

LORD, Power of My Salvation, after many weeks of anticipation, I am about to make my triumphal entrance into the arms of my parents. How I've longed for this moment to come. I am ready! Fifteen percent of my body is stored fat.

Since I haven't yet learned to shiver, the stored fat helps regulate my temperature. My chest sticks out as one who is showing off, proud of whom he is. My lungs will continue developing until the moment of birth. They are producing large quantities of surfactant to keep the air sacs open. I continue to grow; my hair and nails are also growing. Maybe you should make an appointment with the barber or stylist. You will also need to give me a good manicure to prevent me from scratching my face.

I hope that pretty soon you'll see me and I'll see both of you. My Creator knows the precise moment of my birth. Doctors state that a pregnancy can last from 40 to 42 weeks. How I long for that moment to come! I yearn to leave my little house, feel your arms around me, and enjoy your care, as we fall in love with each other.

Prayer Guide for the Physical Development of Our Baby

Oh God, LORD, power of our salvation, you have covered our baby and prepared him for the precise moment when we'll have him in our arms. In you we have put our delight, and have entrusted our baby's journey into our arms. We trust in you and believe you will give us the petitions of our hearts. We know we can do nothing without you. You are the true vine and we are the branches. He who remains in you, and you in him, will bear much fruit, because separated from you, we can do nothing. However, if we remain rooted in your Word, everything we ask will be done.

During this waiting period, neither fear nor discouragement will take hold of us, for you will strengthen us, certainly you will help us, yes, you will sustain us with the justice of your right hand. Your Word establishes that he who dwells in the shelter of the Most High will abide in the shadow of the Almighty. You are our refuge and strength, he in whom we trust. The LORD is our refuge; the Most High is our dwelling place. No evil will harm us, nor will any plague come near us. Our trust is in our LORD, power of our salvation, he will sustain us during this last waiting period. We shall wait upon him with patience, knowing his Word establishes that anyone who believes and says to the mountain "be taken up and cast into the sea" and does not doubt in his heart, but believes that what he says will come to pass, it shall be granted to him. We, therefore, believe that all of the things we've prayed and asked for have been granted and we have received them.

You designed the woman's body with the ability to conceive and give birth. We believe that just as you determined the time our baby would be conceived; you have also fixed the appropriate time for him to be born. Until that day comes, we will rejoice in the trust that the smallest one will become a thousand and the least one, a mighty nation. You, the LORD, will hasten our baby in its time. Our trust is in you, our strength and safeguard.

You are the one who strengthens the woman and the one who gives strength to the weary and power to the weak and strengthen his vigor. Even though the young may fatigue and get tired, those who wait on the LORD will renew their strength; they will rise up with wings like eagles, they will run and not get tired, they will walk and not become weary. LORD, we believe that at in your time you will give the command for our baby to come to our arms. The voice of our LORD is powerful; the voice of the LORD is majestic. The God of glory thunders, the LORD is upon the many waters. In the name of Jesus, we pray. Amen!

Prayer Guide for the Soul of Our Baby (emotions – mind – will)

We worship you, our deliverer, our fortress, our God and rock in whom we take refuge, our shield, the horn of our salvation, our high stronghold. Father, your Word establishes that children are a gift of the LORD; the fruit of the womb is a reward. We thank you for this gift you have given us, to care and raise him in your fear.

In your hand is the life of every living thing, and the spirit of all mankind. We know you have plans for his life, plans for wellbeing and not for calamity, to give him a future and a hope. We ask that, just as you have been our rock, you would be his rock and fortress; and for the love of your name, you would lead and guide him on the path of self-control, like you did with Shadrach, Meshach, and Abed-nego. So, when he searches for you with all his heart, he finds you and has the confidence of knowing that if he asks anything according to your will, you will hear and will grant his petitions. If your answer is delayed, he will know how to wait for you, casting all his anxieties upon you, knowing that you will take care of him. May he understand, just as Shadrach, Meshach and Abed-nego, that this is how the man who fears the LORD is blessed. Even at night, Father we ask you to counsel him and instruct his heart; may his delight be to do your will, for your law is in his heart. May he call upon your name and with songs of praise make known your deeds among the people. May he speak of all your wonders, give glory to your holy name, proclaim the good news of the gospel and never restrain his lips from worshiping you. Hallelujah. In the name of Jesus, we pray. Amen!

Prayer Guide for the Spirit of Our Baby

Our beloved baby, we address your spirit in the name of Jesus of Nazareth. Listen with your spirit to what the Word of God says about you: "And all your sons will be taught by the LORD; and the peace of your sons will multiply." Therefore, spirit of our baby, "rise, shine; for your light has come, and the glory of the LORD has risen upon you. For behold, darkness will cover the earth and deep darkness the nations; but the LORD rises upon you and his glory will appear upon you."

By the delegated authority God has given us as your parents, we establish that as John the Baptist and Samuel were consecrated to God from their mother's womb, and fulfilled their destiny in God, you will fulfill yours. You will proclaim the name of the LORD and the greatness of our God. Baby, you are his workmanship, created in Christ Jesus to do good deeds, which God prepared beforehand so you would walk in them. Your heavenly father made you unique; there is no one like you.

We are convinced that he who began a good work in you will perfect it until the day of Christ Jesus. We prophesy that the Holy Spirit will reveal to you, your identity in God. You will know that you shall be the head and not the tail and you will always be above and never underneath, for you will listen to the commandments of the LORD your God and carefully obey them.

We prophesy all the teachings you have received from your mother's womb have been woven into each part of your being to completely sanctify you, spirit, soul and body, to preserve you without blame for the coming of our LORD, Jesus Christ. You will see yourself as God sees you, perfectly equipped with everything you need to fulfill your purpose in God and cause a lasting impact in the lives of all those around you; because, you are filled with the Word and your spirit constrains you. In the name of Jesus, we pray. Amen!

The Day of Birth – The Parents Speak to Their Baby

Hello, baby! Everything seems to indicate the day has come for your travel through the birth canal and arrival into our arms. Our beloved, don't be afraid of taking this trip, for God is with you. He will strengthen you; certainly he will help you and uphold you with the right hand of his justice. When you pass through the waters, he will be with you, shepherding and directing your path into our arms. While it is true that the process of birthing is a painful one, yet the joy of seeing you will erase from our mind all memory of the birthing pains. Come, come soon into our arms, beloved baby.

Prayer of Confidence by the Mother

The LORD is my shepherd, I shall not want. My God has given orders to his angels concerning me, to guard me at all times. He makes me lie down in green pastures; beside still waters he leads me. He restores my soul; he guides me in the paths of righteousness for his name's sake. Even though I walk through the valley of the shadow of death, I fear no evil, for you are with me; your rod and your staff comfort me; you prepare a table before me in the presence of my enemies, you have anointed my head with oil, my cup overflows. Surely goodness and mercy will follow me all the days of my life and I will dwell in the house of the LORD forever. In the name of Jesus, I pray. Amen!

Prayer of Confidence by the Father

Father, I thank you for the care you have given to my wife and baby. At this time, I present myself as the priest that intercedes for my wife and our baby. I declare you are our keeper, and that with your feathers you cover them and under your wings they find refuge; for your faithfulness is our shield and protection. We ask that since you don't get tired or weary, you give strength and vigor to my wife during the birthing process. Produce in her new strength, a strength propitious to the labor of birthing. Extend your wings over her, our baby, and all the people assisting her. Deposit of your intelligence upon them. Allow me to be an instrument of your peace, give me words to comfort and encourage her. In the name of Jesus, I pray. Amen!

Parents Prayer for When the Contractions Begin

LORD, everything indicates that the moment we have longed for has arrived; the contractions have begun. You are our Alpha and Omega and our trust is in you, and only you. As you guarded his conception and development, you will guard his birth. We know that from the moment of conception, you have possessed our baby. You have kept him in the secret of his mother's womb, but very soon you will let us see his precious countenance and hear his sweet voice. You are our helper; we will fear no evil.

You created the body of the woman and carefully designed it with the ability to conceive and to give birth. Beloved Alpha and Omega, we ask that simultaneously with the intensification of each contraction, a song rise up in our hearts which will gradually raise our confidence in you, our helper. May our voices proclaim that our help comes from the LORD who made the heavens and the earth.

We believe you will not allow anything bad to occur, for the one who guards the process of birthing will not slumber nor sleep. The LORD is our keeper; the LORD is our shadow on our right hand. The LORD will protect us from all evil; he will keep our souls. Even before there's a word in our mouth, behold, oh LORD, you already know it.

We know that soon the labor pains will multiply and with pain our baby will be born. Like the moaning of a dove, perhaps groaning of pain may be heard, yet our eyes will continue to look longingly to the heights, to our LORD, our helper. In the name of Jesus, we pray. Amen!

Parents Prayer During Contractions

You are the great Shepherd that has kept closed the birth canal. You are the gatekeeper that will direct our baby to our arms in the same manner a gatekeeper opens the gate so his sheep can come in and go out. You will call our baby by his name and he will know your voice, just like when you call your sheep by their name and they recognize your voice. You will go before him, guarding his path. For in you is the fountain of life; in your light we see the light of childbirth. Because you are our Alpha and Omega, for the love of your name, you will conduct and guide the process of childbirth. We will not fear because you are with us; from the east you will bring our offspring and from the west you will gather us. You will say to the north: "give them up" and to the south: "do not hold them back." "Bring my sons from afar and my daughters from the ends of the earth." So it will happen on the day of the birth of our baby; you will take our baby out of his mother's womb and cause him to trust, when upon his mother's breast. We will dedicate our baby to you from his birth; from his mother's womb, you are his God. We will exclaim: our child is born; a child has been given to us! Like a shepherd pastures his flock and in his arms gathers his lambs, and in his bosom carries them, we believe you care for the women in labor, until she gives birth. For you will give the order to your angels to keep her and our baby in their path. In the name of Jesus, we pray. Amen!

Appendix

The Baby Who Was
Not Initially Wanted

Be assured that the God of all grace, will perfect, confirm, strengthen and establish in your life and in the life of your baby a new beginning.

1 Peter 5:10 (paraphrased by author)

This section is for parents that upon learning that they have conceived a child, one or both didn't like the idea of having a baby and considered an abortion or tried to abort the baby. There are many circumstances when a baby may not initially be wanted. The news of a pregnancy may evoke adverse and mixed emotions in a couple, emotions that could have even made them consider having an abortion.

Multiple studies have shown that in an unexplainable way, the baby in the mother's womb can perceive if it is wanted or not. With this in mind, I have included what I consider to be a powerful tool to heal this sad beginning and change the future of the baby, your baby, about to be born.

To admit these feelings is not easy, but very necessary. It is indispensable that you confront this situation. You must be honest and make a firm decision to take the important step of dealing with this reality. Our intention is not to create more guilt. On the contrary, our goal is to help set you free, so your baby can feel loved and accepted. What follows is a guide on how to do this in a simple and powerful way!

First step: Face your feelings

Regardless of how the pregnancy came about, the first step is to open your heart before God and present your situation. The following table will serve as a guide. In addition, you can consider having someone help and support you with this process.

Pregnancy: Within Marriage	Pregnancy: Outside of Marriage	Pregnancy: As a result of any type of Sexual Aggression
1. Repent for not wanting your baby.	1. Repent of your sin.	1. Open your heart to God. Tell him about your present situation and ask for His help.
2. Confess your feelings to God.	2. Confess your sin to God.	2. Forgive your aggressor. (Simply say you forgive, even if you don't feel like doing it.)
3. Ask for forgiveness with a sincere heart.	3. Ask for forgiveness with a sincere heart.	3. Ask God to fill you with love for your baby.
4. Thank God for your baby.	4. Thank God for your baby.	4. Thank God for your baby.

Second: Accept the forgiveness of God.

Make the firm decision to believe God and not your emotions.

Have the conviction that our God, whose name is Holy, dwells with the repentant and humble of spirit to revive the spirit of the humble and repentant heart.

Third: Speak to the baby's spirit.

The Bible teaches that the breath of God is the one that imparts life. Your baby already has a spirit inside of his being. Given that the human spirit does not depend on neurological connections, our recommendation is that you speak directly to the spirit of your baby.

Begin by asking forgiveness for having exposed him to the perception that he was not wanted and the pain it caused him. Immediately tell him that you love him and want him. Talk to him about his identity in God and bless him with heavenly blessings.

Model Prayer

(Note: This prayer can be used by either one or both parents.)

Baby, in the name of Jesus Christ, I direct my voice to your spirit. Listen with your spirit to what I have to tell you. I want you to forgive me for the pain I caused you when you perceived that I didn't want you. It was not my intention to hurt you in any way. I want to tell you that I was mistaken. You are not an accident or a mistake. You are a beautiful blessing of God. You were formed by Him and I thank Him for you. Spirit of my baby listen carefully: You are very special, I love you, I desire you and have no doubt that you come to me as a beautiful gift from our heavenly father and bring joy to my heart and His.

Baby, God made you special. You have been designed, molded and created by Him. You are unique. There is no one like you. I need you. The world needs you; you will come to this world with a purpose. You are not an accident, but are a part of the plan of our heavenly father who has designed your spiritual inheritance and has equipped you with everything you will need to fulfill your assignment in this world.

Spirit of my baby, in the name of Jesus, I repeat that I love you and I want you with all of my being. I bless you with a beginning saturated with my love and the love of God. I bless you with spiritual, emotional and physical health. I bless you, my baby, with the conviction that you are wanted and are loved very much. In the name of Jesus, I bless you with the protection of assigned angels for your care from your conception until the very last day of your life. In the precious name of Jesus, I pray. Amen!

When You Have Lived
The Experience of An Abortion

"Hear my voice when I call, O Lord; be merciful to me and answer me."

Psalm 27:7

"You will surely forget your trouble, recalling it only as waters gone by."

Job 11:16

"As a father has compassion on his children, so the Lord has compassion on those who fear him; for he knows how we are formed, he remembers that we are dust."

Psalm 103:13-14

The effect of abortion can leave very deep scars in the body of a woman. A woman's psychological and physical health is affected by the abortion of the child that will always be, for her, throughout her entire life, the baby she never held in her arms. The symptoms of remorse will last for many years. This is because abortion violates the natural order of the emotional reality of a woman. To attempt to ignore the effects of an abortion is the worst mistake a woman can make. A woman, above all, has to face her reality and seek the forgiveness of God to find release from the effects of guilt.

To help you work with the sense of guilt and all the related emotions, I have included a simple guide to assist you.

Guide:

1. Repent. Tell God that you are sorry for having aborted your baby.
2. Accept the fact that God is a forgiving God and no longer remembers our sins.
3. Ask your baby to forgive you for having caused his death. Talk to him as if he were next to you.
4. Forgive those who in one way or another may have pressured you into having
5. the abortion.
6. Forgive the medical staff that participated in the procedure.
7. Close this chapter of your life. You can do this by praying as follows:

Loving Father, thank you for forgiving me for my sin of abortion. Thank you for removing this heavy burden from me and for healing my spirit, my soul and my body from the devastating effects of abortion.

Loving Father, I present to you the baby I aborted. I ask that you let him know that I am repentant for what I did. I am glad to know you received him into your arms, and that your love is more than sufficient. With this prayer, I say good bye to my baby, and with your help I close this chapter of my life. In the name of Jesus, I pray. Amen!

The Loss of Your Baby

"For in the day of trouble he will keep me safe in his dwelling; he will hide me in the shelter of his tabernacle and set me high upon a rock."

Psalm 27:5

"And the God of all grace, who called you to his eternal glory in Christ, after you have suffered a little while, will himself restore you and make you strong, firm and steadfast."

1ˢᵗ Peter 5:10

Statistics indicate that a woman who is healthy and cares for herself during pregnancy has a 10% possibility of losing her baby during the first 10 weeks and less than 5% until the twelfth week. Losses after the third month are less frequent.

Little does it matter in what week the loss of the baby occurs; it still entails a terrible emotional trauma. In the majority of cases, there is no warning or preparation time. The loss is unexpected and heartbreaking. Illusions suddenly turn into a deep sadness and an inexplicable emptiness. The mixture of a heartrending pain, a sense of guilt, fear, anger with your doctor, with God and with the baby for having left, are just a handful of emotions that the mother will have to face and also to a lesser degree, the father.

Each one of these emotions has to be confronted with great courage. With this in mind, I have included a simple guide to assist you in this process.

Guide:

1. Ask the Holy Spirit to be present and to manifest the love of Jesus Christ to you, to take you in his arms and strongly embrace you.
2. While in his arms, pour out your heart before him, with the conviction that he will gather up each tear. Talk to him about your disillusion, your sadness and your anger. Tell him about the emptiness you feel in your womb and the pain of never having heard the cry or laughter of your baby.
3. Be assured that Jesus understands the pain of death. The Bible tells us that Jesus cried when he was told that his friend Lazarus had died. *(John 11:35)*
4. If you used drugs or did something that you think may have caused your baby harm, ask God and your baby for forgiveness.
5. Make the firm decision to forgive all those who you feel let you down: the doctor, the baby, yourself and even God. It's a question of simply speaking forgiveness, although you may not feel any desire to do it.
6. Imagine having your baby in your arms. Talk to him and tell him everything you wanted to tell him but couldn't.
7. Say good bye to your baby with the conviction that he is in heaven being cared for by God; and one day you will see him again.
8. Renounce all feelings of guilt, sadness, disillusion or any other emotions tormenting you.
9. Renounce the fear of losing another baby.
10. Ask God to heal you and fill you with his peace.

Quick Reference

Month 1

Week	Name of God	Bible Character	Prayer Focus The Soul	Prayer Focus The Spirit
1.	Creator	Jesus, the Messiah	N/A	N/A
2.	The Highest	Isaac	N/A	N/A
3.	The Potter	Elizabeth	Fruit of Love	Identity in God
4.	The Good Shepherd	Jonathan	Fruit of Love	Identity in God

Month 2

Week	Name of God	Bible Character	Prayer Focus The Soul	Prayer Focus The Spirit
5.	Shield	John the Baptist	Fruit of Joy	God's Protection
6.	A Jealous God	Shiprah and Puah	Fruit of Joy	Inheritance in God
7.	LORD of the Heavenly Host	Phillip	Fruit of Joy	Identity in God
8.	The LORD Sanctifies	Simeon	Fruit of Joy	Identity in God

Month 3

Week	Name of God	Bible Character	Prayer Focus The Soul	Prayer Focus The Spirit
9.	God Almighty	Abigail	Fruit of Peace	Identity in God
10.	God of All Flesh	Daniel	Fruit of Peace	Identity in God
11.	Adonai	Esther	Fruit of Peace	Identity in God
12.	Faithful and True	Eunice	Fruit of Peace	Spiritual Senses
13.	Jehovah, Shalom	Jael	Fruit of Peace	Spiritual Senses

Month 4

Week	Name of God	Bible Character	Prayer Focus The Soul	Prayer Focus The Spirit
14.	The Lord God	Noah	Fruit of Patience	Spiritual Ears
15.	Eternal God	Job	Fruit of Patience	Spiritual Ears
16.	Faithful and True	Hannah	Fruit of Patience	Spiritual Ears
17.	Creator	Zachariah	Fruit of Patience	Intimacy with God

Month 5

Week	Name of God	Bible Character	Prayer Focus The Soul	Prayer Focus The Spirit
18.	Lord of Heaven	Barnabas	Fruit of Kindness	Identity in God
19.	Banner	Shunammite	Fruit of Kindness	Spiritual Senses
20.	Our Shepherd	John	Fruit of Kindness	Quickened
21.	Our Strength	Ruth	Fruit of Kindness	Strengthened in God

Month 6

Week	Name of God	Bible Character	Prayer Focus The Soul	Prayer Focus The Spirit
22.	Our Righteousness	Dorcas	Fruit of Goodness	Identity
23.	Gentle Breeze	The Centurion	Fruit of Goodness	Armor
24.	Ancient of Days	Joseph of Arimathea	Fruit of Goodness	Belt of Truth
25.	Rock of Israel	Rahab	Fruit of Goodness	Belt of Truth
26.	Strong Tower	Josiah	Fruit of Goodness	Breastplate of Righteousness

Month 7

Week	Name of God	Bible Character	Prayer Focus The Soul	Prayer Focus The Spirit
27.	God of Seeing	Abraham	Fruit of Faithfulness	Footwear of the Gospel of peace
28.	Father	Joshua	Fruit of Faithfulness	The Shield of Faith
29.	Redeemer	Mary, the Mother of Jesus	Fruit of Faithfulness	The Helmet of Salvation
30.	I AM WHO I AM	Jehosheba	Fruit of Faithfulness	Sword of the Spirit

Month 8

Week	Name of God	Bible Character	Prayer Focus The Soul	Prayer Focus The Spirit
31.	The Rock	Jesus	Fruit of Humbleness	Prayer
32.	Holy One of Israel	Samuel	Fruit of Humbleness	Present the gifts of the Holy Spirit. Gift of Wisdom
33.	Eternal God	Moses	Fruit of Humbleness	Gift of Knowledge
34.	Sun of Righteousness	John the Baptist	Fruit of Humbleness	Gift of Faith
35.	God that does Miracles	Joseph, Mary's husband	Fruit of Humbleness	Gift of Healing

Month 9

Week	Name of God	Bible Character	Prayer Focus The Soul	Prayer Focus The Spirit
36.	Our Redeemer	David	Fruit of Self-Control	Gift of Miracles
37.	LORD of Lords	Timothy	Fruit of Self-Control	Gift of Prophecy
38.	Arm of The LORD	Lot	Fruit of Self-Control	Gift of Discernment of Spirits
39.	The LORD is Present	Joseph, son of Jacob	Fruit of Self-Control	Various Kinds of Tongues Interpretation of Tongues
40.	Power of My Salvation	Shadrach, Meshach and Abed-nego	Fruit of Self-Control	Consecrated from the Womb
Birth	Alpha and Omega	N/A	N/A	N/A

Bible Verse Reference

First Month

Week 1
Eph 1:4, 2:10; Rom 4:17; Jer 1:5; Ps 139:15; Heb 2:10; John 15:5; Rom 12:1; 1 John 1:7; Ps 51:10; Deut 7:14; Ps 23:5, 51:10; Eph 3:20; Is 49:16; Gen 1:28a, 30:22; Ps 127:3; Deut 28:2, Is 26:1

Week 2
Ps 145:19; Gen 1:28; Hab 2:3; Is 55:8-9; Matt 7:7-11; Is 26:3; 1 John 4:18; Eccl 3:11; John 15:5; Ps 43:5; Phil 1:6; Rom 8:31; Ex 23:26; Eph 1:20; Matt 10:26; Ps 112:7; Deut 28:12; Is 55:8; Mark14:38; Is 41:10; 2 Cor 10:5; Ps 62:5, 57:2, 2 Pet 3:14; Gen 49:25; Ps 141:3; Col 1:11

Week 3
Is 64:8; Job 33:4; Eph 2:10; Ps 139:13-17, 40:5, 139:11-13, 45:1; Prov 4:23; Deut 6:5; Prov 4:11; Zech 12:1; Gen 1:26- 27, 31; John 8:12; Prov 20:27; 1 Cor 2:11; 1 Pet 2:9; John 16:7; 13; Jer 31:12

Week 4
Ps 23:1,3; Matt 13:32; Ps 16:11; Is 40:11; 2 Tim 3:3; Deut 33:12; Ps 23:1-2, 139:3, 16, 1:3; Jer 18:6b; Is 49:1; 1 John 1:7b; Ezek 37:7; 1 Sam16:7; Ps 33:15; Prov 4:23; Ps 119:103,173, 175; Ps 22:10; Is 26:4; Deut 4:29, Ps 51:6, 58:3; Job 22:25-27; Deut 10:12; Gen 1:27; Jer 1:5; Is 55:9; Ps 91:11-12; 1 Pet 3:4

Second Month

Week 5

Ps 3:3, 139:13; Job 8:7; Ps 139:23; Prov 4:23; Ex 28:28; Job 33:4; Ps 18:33, 91:1-6; 2 Sam 22:31; Luke 1:44; John 6:31, 35, 15:11, 16:22; Acts 2:28; Rom 14:17; Neh 8:9; Is 50:

Week 6

Is 9:7; Ps 119:73a, 129a; Eccl 4:12b; Ps 139:16; Jer 1:9; Is 44:2; 2 Sam 22:34; Luke 1:35a; Col 2:2-4; Eph 1:3-12; Jer 17:7; Rom 12:15; Ps 127:3

Week 7

Ps 31:1, 37:4, 46:7; Neh 2:18; Phil 1:6; Gen 1:12; Ps 19:8; Rom 12:12, 15; Acts 8:26-39; Rom 8:14-17; John 4:24

Week 8

Ex 31:13; Ps 8:3, 2, 22:35, 34:20; Job 8:7; Song 4:1; Ps 119:37; Gen :1:27; Is 43:7; Prov 15:13; Ps 63:7, 59:16;
Luke 2:26-35; Prov 21:1; Is 26:3; Ps 66:17; John 3:16-18; 1 Cor 2:13-16; Dan 11:33; Is 50:4

Third Month

Week 9

Gen 17:1; Acts 7:20; Is 49:16; Eph 6:15, 2:18, 4:3; Matt 5:9; John 16:32-33; Sam 25:3; Deut 10:15; 1 Pet 2:9; Matt 5:14; Job 32:8; 2 Cor 3:18; Eph 4:1; 1 Cor 10:13

Week 10

Jer 32:27; Gen 15:1; Jer 18:6; Song 7:1; Is 55:10-11; Mark 4:20; Ps 49:3, 37:29-31, 32:8, 141:4, 141:3; 2 Chr 17:6; 1 Kin 8:56-58; Job 33:4, 33:6; Gen 1:26, 1:28; Col 1:9

Week 11
Ps 83:18; Gen 1:27-28, 35:11; Job 10:11b, 12a; Luke 2:52; Acts 27:34; Lev 17:11; Ps 119:165, 159, 154, 151, 147-149, 144, 133, 130-131, 127-128, 125, 116-117; 1 Pet 2:2; Job 33:4; Prov 20:27, 23:26

Week 12
Rev 19:11; Ps 139:13; Job 10:8, 8:17a; Is 49:1; Deut 10:17; Jer 31:20; Prov 8:17-20; John 15:1-2, 15:4-5, Luke 24:45; John 14:27; Acts 10:36; Rom 15:33, 13, 14:17-18, 2:18, 8:6, John 6:33; 1 Thess 5:23; Heb 5:14; 2 Tim 3:16, 17; Is 55:10-11

Week 13
Judg 6:24; John 14:27; Job 33:4, 4:12, Ps 19:8b; Song 4:4, 3:8; Ps 5:12; Job 31:27; 1 Thess 5:23-24; Job 11:17-18; Ps 27:3-4; Eph 2:14; 1 Cor 14:33; Rom 16:20; 2 Thess 3:16; Heb 5:14; Prov 22:6; 2 Tim 3:17, 3:14; Eccl 3:10-11;
Is 48:17; 2 Tim 4:2

Fourth Month

Week 14
Gen 2:4; Luke 1:35; 1 Cor 6:18–20; Eccl 11:5; Ex 34:29; Ps 37:7-9; Rom 12:1-2; Gen 6:13; Heb 11:6; Eph 1:18-19; Rom 15:4-5; Heb 10:36; John 10:27; Rom 10:17; Job 29:21; Acts 4:24

Week 15
Deut 33:7; Rom 5:3-5; Ps 37:24; Eccl 7:8; Deut 33:27; Ps 91:1; Ezek 12:2; Eccl 7:5; Ps 143:8,10; Is 143:9

Week 16
Rev 1:5; Ps 33:15; Job 27:3; Song 4:4; 1 Sam 1:6; Prov 3:11-12; Is 30:15, 48:17; Rev 1:6; Ezek 3:10; Luke 24:45; Rom 12:2; Ps 3:3

Week 17

Gen 1:27; Song 1:17; Ps 139:15; Josh 2:18; Is 66:14; Luke 1:6; Prov 4:20-27; Is 11:1; John 15:9-11; 1 Cor 1:5, 7-9; Eph 3:16-19

Fifth Month

Week 18

Ps 7:10, 138:1, 8:2, 51:10; Zeph 3:17; Amos 4:13; Matt 8:22; Ps 19:8b; Gen 35:11; Ps 1:3; 1 Tim 1:5; Eph 5:11-3, 5:10; Acts 4:36, 11:24, 9:27; 2 Thess 1:11-12; Is 54:13; 3:10-12

Week 19

Ex 17:15; Matt 10:30; Ex 17:5; Ps 4:8; Job 10:8; Gen 1:27; Ps 128:3; Song 4:2; Heb 4:16; Gal 5:22; Matt 13:8; 2 Kin 4:13; Rom 12:3; Is 48:17, 42:6-7; Ex 17:15; Matt 18:8; 1 Cor 1:5, 2:9-10; 2 Tim 1:13-15, 2:22; 1 Cor 2:13

Week 20

Ps 23:1, 8:4-6, 121:7; Prov 14:30a; Phil 1:6; Ex 35:21; 2 Tim 4:17a; Job 12:11b; Gen 27:21; Ps 94:9; Gen 9:7; Rom 10:17; Ps 145:21; Prov 4:23, 4:20, 4:25, 4:27; Col 3:10, 3:12-15; Job 32:8; Ezek 36:27; Ps 119:133; 1 Cor 2:11; Is 54:13

Week 21

Ps 22:19; Rom 8:39; Gal 1:15; 16, Prov 14:30; Eph 4:29-30, 5:1-2, 19-20; 2 Cor 10:5; Eph 6:10-12; Heb 4:12; Mat 24:12; Col 1:12; Prov 20:27; Is 60:1; 1 John 1:5; Job 12:22

Sixth month

Week 22

Jer 33:16; Is 49:1; Deut 21:12; Is 44:24; 42:6; Prov 4:13, 5; Song 4:15; Prov 4:22; Ps 1:3, 89:14; Col 3:18; 1 Tim 1:5; Rom 15:14; Mal 3:18;

James 1:22, 27; Acts 9:36; 1 Cor 6:20; Jer 33:20, 21; Ps 95:7; Luke 1:80; Rom 13:12; 2 Cor 10:3, 4

Week 23
1 Kin 19:12; Is 43:21, 50:5; Col 2:19b; Job 40:16; Matt 8: 5-6, 8; Ps 86:15; Prov 2:1-6; 1 Kin 19:12-14; Eph 2:13; Deut 8:4; 1 John 4:4

Week 24
Dan 7:9; 2 Cor 2:14-15; Ps 102:27; 1 Thess 3:11; Is 46:4; Ps 63:8, 16:11; Heb 13:5; Matt 27:57-60; Acts 20:35; Eph 6:14; John 3:16, 14:6; 1 Cor 2:14; John 14:20, 21; Eph 1:21; Gen 1:26; Song 4:1, 5:14-16

Week 25
Dan 7:9; 2 Cor 2:14; Ps 102:27; 1 Thess 3:11; Is 46:4; Ps 63:8, 16:11; Heb 13:5; Matt 27:57, 59-60; Acts 20:35; Eph 6:14; John 3:16, 14:6; 1 Cor 2:14; John 14:20-21; Eph 1:21; Gen 1:26; Song 4:1, 5:14-16

Week 26
Prov 18:10; Song 7:4; Ps 119:18; John 8:12; Job 26:13; Ps 19:8, 145:5-12, 119:5-7, 119:10-11; Gen 24:18-22; Eph 6:14; Rom 3:24; Jer 17:9; Prov 27:19, 4:23; 2 Kin 22:1-2; Prov 23:26; 2 Cor 1:21-22; Ps 37:31, 40:8, 51:10, 86:11, 119:34, 111-112

Seventh Month

Week 27
Gen. 15:20-21; Deut 34:7; 2 Sam 14:25; Gen 12:14, 2:7; Deut 7:15; 1 Sam 3:10; Prov 23:16, 2:6; Gen 16:13; Ps 141:8; Rev 4:11; 1 Sam 2:35; Neh 9:7-8; Eph 6:19-20; 1 Cor 1:18; Eph 1:3-6, 6:15; John 14:27

Week 28

2 Sam 7:14; Eccl 11:5; Ps 139:13-15; Ps 141:8; Job 38:36; 2 Sam 14:26; Ps 28:7; Song 2:4; Is 63:16; Ps 119:114-116; Col 3:2; Ps 119:174; Luke 24:45; Col 3:3-5; Ps119:173, 172, 175; Eph 6:16; Rom 10:17; Rom 1:17; 2 Cor 5:7; 2 Sam 22:31; Ps 3:3; Ps 115:11,13; Heb 11:6; Rom 4:18, 21, 22

Week 29

Job 19:25; Ps 119:73; Gen 2:7; 2 Kin 6:17; John 3:21; 8:12; Ps 119:131; Job 34:3; Ps 119:103; 2 Cor 2:14-15; Ps 84:5; Prov 2:1; 1 Tim 3:14-17; Is 50:4; Ps 19:14; 2 Cor 2:15; Prov 2:10; Ps 24:6, 19:7-8; Heb 8:10; Job 19:25; Heb 8:10-12; Matt 26:28; Eph 6:17, 4:24; 2 Cor 11:3b; John 14:18,16

Week 30

Ex 3:14; 2 Sam 22:31; Zeph 3:17; Is 25:8a; Ps 23:5b; 2 Tim 3:16; Ex 3:14-15; Is 55:11; Ps 19:9-14; 2 Kin 11:2-3; Eph 6:17; Heb 4:12; Ps 1:1-2, 119:53, 55, 62, 60, 63

Eight Month

Week 31

Gen 49:24; Luke 2:40, 1:80; Job 40:18; Jer 31:13a; Is 54:13; Prov 8:14; Ps 16:5, 11; Gal 5:22-23; Col 3:12-13; 1 Pet 3:15-17; Eph 4:1-3; 1 Cor 2:13; Eph 6:18; 1 John 5:14; Is 45:11; 1 Pet 2:5; Ps 119:149; Matt 6:6-7; 2 Chr 7:1, 3

Week 32

Ps 71:22; Ex 15:1; Song 6:10, 7:1-5, 5:12-16, 4:1, 3-5; Is 54:13; Ps 66:9; Eph 3:12; Ps 51:10, 108:1, 138:8, 14-15; 1 Sam 2:26; Jer 17:5, 24:7; Eph 4:17-19; 1 Cor 12:1, 4-11, 14:39; 1 Tim 5:19, 4:14; 2 Tim 1:6

Week 33

Is 40:28-31; Ex 29:6; Is 54:13; Ps 36:6, 8-9; 2 Sam 22:16; Ps 28:8; 1 Sam 2:9; Ps 28:9, 84:5; 1 Cor 15:49, 10:13, 12:8; Hos 4:6; Dan 2:29; Rev 21:6; Job 12:22; 1 Cor 4:1; Gen 18:17a

Week 34

Mal 4:2; Is 62:3; Ps 19:8; Ex 33:7, 11; Ps 84:11; Gen 49:25b; Ps 22:9; Is 42:6; Job 37:16; Deut 29:29; Ps 84:2, 4-6, 8-9; Eph 1:18; John 3:28, 30; Matt 5:5; 1 Cor 12:8-9; Heb 11:6; Rom 12:3; Matt 17:20; 1 Cor 2:4-5

Week 35

Ps 77:14; John 16:21; Ps 138:2; Job 36:10, 38:36; Prov 2:9-13; Col 3:2; 1 Cor 12:7:9; Ex 15:26; Jer 33:6; Mark 16:17-18; Acts 19:12

Ninth Month

Week 36

Is 60:16; Ps 31:3; Job 12:10; Ps 139:13; Job 10:9-12; Ps 18:32, 31:15, 37:3-7, 23, 31, 51:15, 119:14; Gen 18:14; Ps 10:17; Gal 5:22-23; 1 Cor 12:7-8, 10; Gen 1; Ex 14:21-22; Dan 6:22, 5:5; John 2:7-11; Matt 14:13-21; Heb 13:8; John 14:12-13; Ps 37:4-5; 1 Cor 1:6, 2:11, 14:1; Ps 42:1

Week 37

Deut 10:17; John1:9; Ps 18:35; Prov 3:16; Job 29:15; Eccl 3:11a; Ps 66:5, 18:35; Gal 1:15-16; Job 23:11; Phil 2:13; Ps 119:10-12, 15:20; 1 Cor 12:7-8, 10, 14:3, 1; Is 55:11; Prov 22:17; John 14:26; Col 1:12; Acts 2:18

Week 38

Is 53:1; Ps 121:8, 4-5, 7; Matt 10:30; Ps 121:2-3, 41:2; 1 Kin 3:9; Gen 18:20; Is 3:9; Ps 42:1, 63:1; John 16:8; 2 Pet 2:9, 7-8; Ps 84:2; 1 Cor 12:8 10; Luke 4:33; Gen 22:11; Dan 2:1; Rom 5:20; Mal 3:18

Week 39

Ezek 48:35; Job 33:4; Phil 1:6; Heb 4:3; Jer 1:12; Heb 4:12a; Is 55:11; 2 Sam 22:31a; Jer 29:12, 14a; 1 John 5:15; Matt 7:7; Eccl 3:1; Jer 29:10-11; Ps 41:2; 1 Pet 5:7; Phil 1:6; Ps 16:9, 66:9, 121:7, 31:3, 138:3, 7-8, 143:6, 77:12; Gal 5:24; Ps 119:36-37; Matt 6:22; Ps 119:38; 1 Cor 12:8, 10; Mark 16:17; Acts 2:4; 1 Cor 13:1, 14:2; Rom 8:26; 1 Cor 14:13-14; John 3:34; Rom 8:15

Week 40

Ps 140:7, 37:4-6; John 15:4, 7; Is 41:10; Ps 91:1-2, 9-10; Mark 11:23-24; Judg 13:5; Eccl 3:11, 2,12; Is 60:22; Ps 28:8; Is 40:29–31; Ps 29:4, 3, 9, 18:2, 127:3; Job 12:10; Jer 29:11; Ps 31:3; Jer 29:13; 1 John 5:14-15, 7; Ps 128:4, 16:7, 40:8; 1 Cor 16:8-10; Ps 40:9; Is 54:13, 60:1-2; Deut 32:3; Eph 2:10; Phil 1:6; Deut 28:13; 1 Tim 5:23; Job 32:18

Labor

Is 41:10, 43:2; John 16:21; Ps 23: 1, 91:11, 23: 2-6, 121:8; Prov 8:22; Song 2:14; Ps 121:1-5, 7, 139:4; Gen 3:16; Is 38:14; John 10:3-4, Ps 36:9, 31:3; Is 43:5-6; Luke 2:6; Ps 22:9-10; Is 9:6, 40:11; Is 9:6; Ps 91:11; 2 Tim 1:7